the IngramSpark®

Guide to Independent Publishing

by Brendan Clark

GRAPHIC ARTS
BOOKS®

Library of Congress Control Number: 2015950546

ISBN: 978-1-943328-35-2 (pbk.)
ISBN: 978-1-943328-48-2 (hardbound)
ISBN: 978-1-943328-45-1 (e-book)

Edited by Robin Cutler
Designed by Vicki Knapton

Published by Graphic Arts Books
An imprint of

GRAPHIC ARTS
BOOKS®
P.O. Box 56118
Portland, Oregon 97238-6118
503-254-5591
www.graphicartsbooks.com

CONTENTS

INTRODUCTION

Publishing: Traditional vs Independent

To the delight of authors everywhere, recent advances in print-on-demand technology have lowered the cost of short-run book manufacturing and made the opportunity of independently publishing oneself accessible to thousands of writers. The practice of "indie" publishing has been employed to great success throughout literary history (e.g. Mark Twain, Beatrix Potter, Stephen King, Barbara Freethy, and Hugh Howey, among many others), yet within the past several decades, it has been prohibitively difficult for authors to distribute their books on a national level, unless they have been signed by an established publishing house.

In most cases, traditional publishing requires a process of submitting one's manuscript to agents, who in turn pitch the manuscript to acquisitions editors at publishing houses. Once the book has been accepted, the publisher invests in the cost of editing, designing, producing, marketing, and distributing the book. Authors who choose to publish themselves essentially shoulder the responsibility and costs for all of these tasks. In exchange, indie authors retain absolute artistic control, not to mention a higher percentage of the profits from their total book sales.

Don't make the mistake of underestimating the various compounding costs of publishing a book! The process of preparing a manuscript for production, getting it in print, digitizing it as an e-book, and then publicizing it to readers involves a massive investment of time—several months at least, sometimes even a full year. Authors should also be prepared for the financial investment involved in ISBN (see page 56) registration, paying freelancers or service providers for editing and design services, paying a printer for the cost of materials, printing promo materials, hiring publicity agents and website designers, etc.

There's a very good reason entire corporations are built around the process of shepherding a book from its roughest form to bookstore shelves—when done right, it can be a lengthy and expensive process. To deal with these obstacles, publishing houses delegate tasks to skilled professionals with experience in crafting books. Likewise, indie authors would be wise to surround themselves with professionals who specialize in the particular phases of polishing and publicizing books. We'll discuss those professionals, and how to make the most of their services, in later sections of this guide.

Those who have experienced the entirety of this process often draw a startlingly accurate analogy between publishing a book and birthing a child. Both are an arduous, emotional journey, in which months of labor and devotion culminate in the creation of something totally unique. Just like expectant mothers and fathers, authors must exercise a great deal of patience and often endure considerable stress while the development of their manuscript takes place. But just as an infant bears the genetic code of its parents, a finished book bears the artistic signature of its author—no one else could have written your book but you.

Titles published in the traditional fashion typically receive significantly more exposure than indie titles, due to the tremendous marketing efforts of industry professionals and the distribution channels connecting publishers with retailers and the general public. However, truly committed indie published authors can invest in marketing to dramatically enhance the sales potential of their books. There are numerous ways to generate buzz for a new book—hang up posters around town, have an article written about your book in your local newspaper, raise funds through an online crowdfunding campaign like Kickstarter or Inkshares, offer signed copies to folks who preorder the book, make noise on social media, suggest your book to local book groups, and schedule a reading event at your local bookstore. Later on, we'll discuss how national distribution can be essential for reaching distant readers, once your marketing has spread interest in your book beyond your own circle of acquaintances.

Bear in mind that indie publishing should not be viewed as an exclusive alternative, but as a possible step along the path to being traditionally published. Consider how much more impressive a well-edited bound paperback would be than a loose-leaf manuscript in the eyes of an agent. This arrangement is a win for publishing houses as well; in their eyes, an indie book that has already established a readership and demonstrated strong sales is a much safer investment than a totally unproven title that could become either a hit or a flop.

Many excellent books have been written on the general topic of self- and indie publishing. In this book, my goal is to guide you through a uniquely versatile tool for accomplishing your indie publishing goals—IngramSpark.

Welcome to IngramSpark

If you were to ask the employees at almost any bookstore in the United States where the books on their shelves came from, they'd likely tell you that most were ordered from Ingram. Established nearly 50 years ago, Ingram Content Group is the largest book distributor in the world, serving 39,000+ book retailers worldwide, of both the brick-and-mortar and the online variety.

Ingram's primary function is to channel books from publishing houses to retailers, but the distributor also owns the world's most technologically advanced print-on-demand company, Lightning Source, which produces books at multiple facilities around the world. In July of 2013, Ingram introduced IngramSpark as a portal for independent publishers and authors to access its print-on-demand services, print distribution channels, and e-book distribution channels—these complementary functions make IngramSpark a true one-stop platform for publishers who want an easy and comprehensive way to bring their books to a national audience.

Since then, IngramSpark has expanded its services to include resources for editing your manuscript, designing your book, shipping books directly to your customers, and promoting your book to retailers and libraries. Since books uploaded through IngramSpark are entered into the same database as frontlist titles from established publishers, retailers can search for and order these books as they would any other distributed title. When such orders are placed, your book is printed on demand, shipped to the retailer (with the option for trade standard wholesale terms), and sold to readers.

For the next few chapters, I'd like to walk you through the most essential steps to preparing a manuscript for production and discuss how IngramSpark can be utilized effectively for each step; then, we'll explore the process of uploading and managing your titles from the IngramSpark online Dashboard.

While the magnitude and variety of steps involved here may seem intimidating at first, IngramSpark is designed to streamline the process into a sensible order. This book includes a glossary should you encounter any unfamiliar terminology. Also, Ingram's responsive customer support team is available at [www.ingramspark.com/Portal/Help] to answer any questions you might have.

PREPRODUCTION

Editing

Once you've finished writing your manuscript, think of it as a roughly hewn sculpture. The raw materials have been compiled, the basic shape is there, but it takes a great deal of polishing before the project can be considered finished.

In writing, as in life, errors happen to everyone. And anyone who has been working on a manuscript for a long time is much less likely to spot grammatical mistakes than a reader approaching the manuscript for the first time. Seek a fresh set of eyes that can identify errors that the writer's eyes are likely to miss, or that can offer feedback regarding stylistic choices and organization.

Some particularly common errors to watch out for include:

- **Verb tense:** Jump, jumped, jumping, or will jump? Several verb tenses are acceptable depending on what kind of book is being written, but it is essential to keep your verb tense accurate and consistent.

- **Apostrophes:** Be sure to use apostrophes for contractions and posses-

sives, and use no apostrophe for plurals (e.g. "Don't eat Mary's cookies.")
Also, remember that "its" is possessive, while "it's" is a contraction for it is
(e.g. "It's great when a business honors its values").

- **Misspellings**: Keep a dictionary handy. Most publishers use *Merriam-Webster's Collegiate Dictionary*, 10th ed. Or use the Internet, if you prefer.

- **Sentence fragment:** Any sentence that lacks both a subject and a predicate (i.e. an action). For example, "The marathon runner tied his shoes," is a complete sentence, whereas "The marathon runner," and "Tied his shoes," are both sentence fragments.

- **Comma splice:** When two independent clauses are separated by a comma rather than a semicolon or a period.

If any of the terms above sound like gibberish, it would probably be a good idea to enlist the help of an experienced editor. Feedback from family, friends, and neighbors can be a vital aspect of your manuscript's development—that said, professional editors have the skills to root out persistent global errors and hard-to-spot grammatical errors that most folks miss. Don't underestimate the value of a trained outside perspective!

The best way to get on the same page with a freelance editor is to send her or him a small sample of your manuscript (e.g. 10-20 pages) as a test-drive. This way, you can get a sense of the editor's style, ask for a cost estimate using the sample as a point of reference, and identify any issues in the feedback before the editor commits to working on the entire manuscript.

Be sure to communicate clearly regarding the variety of edits your manuscript needs. Freelance editing services will typically fall into one of three categories:

PROOFREADING involves weeding out all typos, misspellings, and punctuation errors. It is the least rigorous editing style, and therefore usually the most affordable.

COPYEDITING often includes correcting line errors, but also addresses formatting issues, fact-checking, and general stylistic consistency.

CONTENT EDITING delves deeper to provide qualitative feedback on the subject matter of a manuscript. In the case of fiction, the editor helps streamline the plot structure, comments on believability, and offers suggestions on various elements of the narrative. For nonfiction, the editor would primarily focus on clarity, flow, and how to most effectively organize the sections of the book. This variety of editing is by far the most intensive, and as such carries the highest price tag.

This stage of the process typically involves a substantial investment of time, but don't get discouraged! Ultimately, your book will be more polished and easier to read as a result of being thoroughly edited. Try inquiring about local editors at any schools, bookstores, or libraries in your area; you can also try the Chamber of Commerce.

Graphic Design

Interior

Designing the physical appearance of your book is another crucial step in the development of your manuscript. Before your book is ready to be printed, its pages must be sized according to the printer's specifications.

If you were to examine a published book, you'll notice that there's more than just text on every page—page numbers, chapter headings, flourishes separating

IngramSpark supports the following book dimensions (in inches):

SMALL FORMAT

4.37×7	5.25×8	5.83×8.27	7.44×9.69
5.06×7.81	5.5×8.25	6.14×9.21	8×8
5×7	5.5×8.5	6.69×9.61	8.5×8.5
5×8	6×9	7.5×9.25	8.5×9

LARGE FORMAT

6.625×10.25	8×10	8.25×11	8.5×11
7×10	8×10.88	8.268×11.693	

For the most up-to-date list of compatible dimensions,
go to ingramspark.com/portal/booktypes.

sections of text, photos, illustrations, page headings with the title and author name—these elements are all added during the design phase. Not only should a reader be able to understand the content you've written, they should also be able to identify where they currently are in your book and be able to clearly see where distinct sections begin and end.

This is also an ideal time to add supplementary content to your book, including a copyright page, dedication page, table of contents, acknowledgments page, references section, and glossary. Though some of these extra pieces are optional for certain varieties of books (especially fiction), several of them provide essential organizational functions. Your copyright page protects your book from plagiarism by

To my friend Dorothy Nicholson, who never once stopped
believing in me, and whom I'll never forget. — P. F.

To Nanette, Marcia, Kaylene, Monica, and Michelle,
who encourage me on the writing journey. — A. D.

▲ *Robert*

Text © 2001 by Pam Flowers and Ann Dixon
All photographs except for the one on page 32 © 2001 by Pam Flowers
Illustration © 2001 by David Totten
Photograph on page 32 is from the book *Across Arctic America* by
Knud Rasmussen, published in 1927 by G.P. Putnam's Sons.

Library of Congress Cataloging-in-Publication Data
Flowers, Pam.
    Alone across the Arctic : one woman's epic journey by dog team / Pam Flowers with
Ann Dixon.
        p.   cm
Includes index.
    ISBN 978-0-88240-836-1 formally published as: 978-0-88240-547-6 (hardbound) —
    ISBN 978-0-88240-539-1 (softbound)
    ISBN 978-1-943328-10-9 (paper over board)
    ISBN 978-1-941821-64-0 (e-book)
1. Flowers, Pam—Journeys—Arctic regions. 2. Flowers, Pam—Journeys—Alaska.
3. Flowers, Pam—Journeys—Canada, Northern. 4. Arctic regions—Description and
travel. 5. Alaska—Description and travel. 6. Canada, Northern—Description and
travel. 7. Dogsledding—Arctic regions. 8. Dogsledding—Alaska. 9. Dogsledding—
Canada, Northern. I. Dixon, Ann. II. Title.
G635. F56 A3 2001
919.804—dc21   2001000636

Alaska Northwest Books®
An imprint of

GRAPHIC ARTS
BOOKS®

P.O. Box 56118
Portland, OR 97238-6118
(503) 254-5591
www.graphicartsbooks.com

Copy Editor: Linda Gunnarson
Design: Constance Bollen, cb graphics
Map: Gray Mouse Graphics

A typical copyright page layout.

CONTENTS

Table of Contents. Typically, only the word "Contents" is used on this page.

For the animals, who enrich our human lives
And for my grandchildren, Tristan and Alyssa

HERBAL DIRECTORY

HERBAL CLASSES, SCHOOLS, APPRENTICE PROGRAMS
California School of Herbal Studies, 9309 California 116, Forestville, California 95436 www.cshs.com
Good Earth Garden School, Ellen Vande Visse, P.O. Box 2905, Palmer, AK. 99645; see www.goodearthgardenschool.com for GEGS classes in organic gardening and communicating with nature and Janice Schofield herbal classes)
SAGE, Rosemary Gladstar, P.O. Box 420, East Barre, Vermont 05649, www.sagemt.com
Sweetgrass School of Herbalism, Robyn Klein, 6101 Shadow Circle Drive, Bozeman, Montana 59715

HERBAL PRODUCTS, FLOWER ESSENCES
Alaskan Flower Essence Project, P.O. Box 1090, Victor, Montana 59875 www.alaskanessences.com
HERB PHARM, P.O. Box 116, Williams, Oregon 97544; www.herb-pharm.com
The Wild'Erb Company, Ohio Valley Herbal Products, Inc. 125 Saint George Street, Suite 5, East Liverpool, OH 43920; www.thewilderbcompany.com
Jean's Greens, 1545 Columbia Turnpike, Schodack, NY 12033; www.jeansgreens.com (herbs, supplies, containers, essential oils)

HERBAL ASSOCIATIONS AND PUBLICATIONS
Alaska Native Plant Society, P.O. Box 141613 Anchorage, AK 99514; native plant walks and newsletter; www.aknps.org
Alaska Mycological Society, P.O. Box 2526, Homer, AK 99603; The Wild Food Forum (quarterly newsletter) www.ecoimages-us.com

SEEDS
Abundant Life Seeds, P.O. Box 157, Saginaw, Oregon 97472; www.abundantlifeseeds.com
Seeds of Change P.O. Box 15700 Sante Fe, New Mexico 87506; www.seedsofchange.com (organically grown and heirloom seeds)

INDEX

Boldface numbers refer to color photographs.

93

Examples of typical front and back matter page layouts. Clockwise from top left: dedication, index, and references pages.

Ownership of intellectual property is automatically implied in the United States. This means that you own all rights to the manuscript you've written, even if you haven't formally registered with the national copyright office. The purpose of your copyright page is to explicitly state your ownership and provide essential data about your book all in one place; it should include something to the effect of "All rights reserved. Copyright © 201X by [insert your name here]. No part of this publication may be reproduced or transmitted in any form or by any means, without permission in writing from the author."

asserting that you maintain exclusive rights to the text, while a references section gives credit to the work of other writers to show that you haven't been guilty of plagiarism yourself. A table of contents helps readers navigate the various sections of your book, while an index helps readers locate particular keywords. If you're unsure about how these elements should appear in a book, just take a look at how they're presented in the book you're currently holding in your hands, or a book on your shelf that is similar to the one you're writing.

The best way to ensure that the visual appearance of your pages encourages smooth reading is to hire a professional graphic designer. Some designers plug the writer's text into a premade template, while others build each book from scratch; in both cases, the designer's primary function is to mold your manuscript from a shapeless text block into an attractively presented, well-organized set of bindable pages. An experienced designer can also give informed recommendations on font choices, line length and spacing, and page margin width, all of which have a massive impact on your book's readability.

Cover

As the outside shell of your book, the cover overwhelmingly determines a potential reader's first impression. Like it or not, people do judge books by their covers. Folks browsing in bookstores are far more likely to pick something up off the shelf if it catches their eyes with an engaging cover (one that "pops," as they say in the book business), while an unattractive cover practically guarantees that your book will remain untouched and undiscovered.

Covers also provide a great deal of functional information. A synopsis on the back, ideally with positive marketing blurbs alongside it, is often the first place readers will look to answer the question of whether a particular book is the sort of book they'd enjoy. An author photo with accompanying bio helps brand your book as yours. In the case of paperbacks, the book's list price should be displayed on the back cover, while most hardcovers display the price on one of the inside flaps of the dust jacket. Finally, a barcode can be easily scanned by retailers for sales and inventory purposes.

Whether you want your book bound in a tastefully minimalist solid color or a multi-layered collage of images and elaborate lettering, professional graphic designers possess the skills and experience to turn your vision into reality. Typically, a designer will confer with the author to discuss the general aesthetic of the cover and to collect any images the author may have compiled for design purposes. Then the designer will build the cover spread and send a draft to the author, making adjustments to the details as needed. Trust me, it's incredible what a graphic designer can do with a few scanned photos and a bit of artistic direction.

Like most print-on-demand binderies, IngramSpark requires that cover files be submitted as a full spread—back cover, spine, and front cover, with a quarter inch of bleed space on all outside edges of the spread. IngramSpark provides you with a helpful template customized to your book's particular size specs and spine width, upon which you superimpose your cover spread before uploading (more on this in the "Title Upload" chapter).

BINDING FORMATS

Black & White vs Color

Throughout the process of crafting your manuscript, it's wise to keep the finished form of your book constantly in the back of your mind. Many indie authors stick to one binding type (e.g. paperback only or e-book only) for simplicity and efficiency. Others emulate the traditional pattern used by major publishing houses—simultaneous hardcover and digital release, followed by paperback release 6 to 12 months later.

If you're unsure of which binding type would be the best fit for your book, consider above all else the preferences of the people who will read your book. One of the many perks of publishing independently is the freedom to mix and match binding types to suit the particular tastes of your audience. Since it can be difficult to know at the outset what formats your readers prefer, it's advisable to choose as many formats as you can afford. Most traditional publishers simultaneously publish their titles in multiple formats—hardcover, paperback, and e-book—all at the same time. With this approach, you know that you're covering your bases; lucky for you, IngramSpark supports all formats.

One of the first decisions you'll need to make is whether the interior of your print book should be produced in black & white or in full color. For novelists and nonfiction writers who don't include images in their text, this should be an easy choice. Black & white print, often called grayscale, is considerably cheaper than color; that said, the cost of color book printing has sharply dropped in recent years, making it increasingly viable for independent publishers. This has been especially good news for authors and illustrators of children's picture books, who can affordably publish their own creations without wading through the particularly competitive kids' book industry. Color printing also opens up opportunities for scientific writers using graphs and diagrams, artists who want to publish a visual gallery of their work in book form, and writers of hybrid books that combine photographs or imagery with poetry or essays.

IngramSpark offers black & white printing on white paper or cream paper, along with color printing at several cost levels. Standard color printing on 70lb white paper achieves a full color effect for minimal expense, while premium color printing on 70lb white paper features more crisp, vibrant, high-quality ink—essential for photo books and books with full-page illustrations.

Paperback

By a long shot, the perfect-bound trade paperback is the most commonly printed book in the indie publishing arena. Its compact, lightweight shape makes it inexpensive to ship, which combined with its modest production cost has made the paperback the print format of choice for any publisher on a budget. Furthermore, many people who habitually read on-the-go prefer paperbacks, since they are more easily portable and are easier to hold on to than heavier books. Perfect binding involves printing the pages with toner or ink and binding the page block to a printed and laminated coverstock with hot glue.

A softbound cover designed using the IngramSpark Cover Template Generator.

Out of all the binding formats, a 6x9 paperback offers the most page area per dollar spent and the least waste of paper in production. That said, the most important consideration when deciding on your final binding specs is what looks and feels right for your book. Since books with smaller page dimensions can hold less text on each page than books with larger page dimensions, the smaller version of a given book will have more total pages than the larger version of that same book. The total number of pages determines a book's spine width, so authors can adjust page size to give their books a thinner or thicker shelf presence.

IngramSpark prints perfect-bound paperbacks in all of the sizes listed under the "Graphic Design" heading (see page 11); feel free to experiment with several potential dimensions when deciding on the right size and width for your book (more on this process under the "Basic Metadata" heading on page 40). Typically, books with fewer pages tend to be published in smaller formats to make them feel more substantial, while books with more pages tend to be published in larger formats to keep the spine from being too thick. In the end, it all comes down to some combination of taste and cost.

An alternative to the perfect-bound paperback for short books (4 to 48 pages) is the saddle stitch paperback, also called booklet or chapbook. These follow the same binding procedure as perfect-bound books, except that the pages are bound to the cover with staples rather than glue. The saddle stitching process saves a great deal of cost in binding, though books printed in this fashion cannot have any spine text.

Because saddle stitch paperbacks cannot be easily identified while spine-out on a shelf, they sell best when featured on a spinner or table display. The chapbook style lends itself particularly to collections of poetry, instruction manuals, or pocket-sized field guides.

Hardcover

The above image shows what the same title would look like as a cased-in binding (left) and a perfect bind (right).

Unlike many print-on-demand services, IngramSpark supports hardcover bookbinding in a variety of sizes, with or without a dust jacket. For traditional publishers, the hardcover represents the flagship edition of a given book; hardcore book collectors pursue first-edition hardcovers above all else. For debut books in most mainstream genres, the hardcover is typically

The same title as show on page 21, but now designed in a cased-in hardbound template. Note the space needed on a hardbound in order to wrap around the board material.

released several months to a year before the paperback, in order to maximize sales to the portion of the market most dedicated to buying that particular title—this practice has become increasingly popular with ambitious indie publishers, thanks in large part to the advent of affordable print-on-demand hardcover binding.

Hardcovers produced by IngramSpark are made in two very similar processes: case binding and cloth binding. In both cases, pages of printed text are combined into a block that is stitched to a rigid cover. The crucial difference is that case bound covers are made of cardboard wrapped in laminated paper that has the cover image printed directly on it, while cloth bound covers are made of cardboard covered

A dust jacket designed using the IngramSpark "cloth binding" Cover Template Generator.

(predictably) in fabric. While the production cost involved may deter some authors, hardcovers should be considered in every way the deluxe version of a book; committed readers are often willing to pay more in exchange for their durability and aforementioned collector's value.

The most obvious example of case bound books are large format hardcover textbooks, along with cookbooks and art anthologies. Sturdy and resistant to shelf wear, this binding style is also perfect for those who approach reading as a form of weight lifting. Case binding can also be used to great effect in small formats such as gift books, novellas, and journals.

Most debut fiction titles first appear on bookstore shelves as a cloth bound hardcover with a dust jacket— likewise for debut titles in the history, biography,

The dust jacket on the final product.

science, and social studies genres. IngramSpark cloth-binds with either blue or gray fabric, with the option of embossing the spine of one's book with the title and author name in gold lettering. The dust jacket wraps around the rigid cover, with inside flaps on the left and right typically used for the book's synopsis and author bio, respectively.

One thing to keep in mind when designing cover images for these formats is the extra bleed space required by hardcover templates, due to the paper cover wrapping around the cardboard coverstock. In the case of cloth bound cover spreads, the extra space afforded by the flaps of the dust jacket gives much more room for extra artwork or positive reviews recommending the book to readers.

E-book

Finally, IngramSpark allows authors to upload the digital edition of their books to a variety of mainline e-book platforms all at once. Once your e-book enters Ingram's distribution channels, it becomes discoverable to readers shopping on Amazon Kindle, Apple iBooks, Barnes & Noble Nook, or Kobo readers.

Many book buyers today use e-readers and tablets as an alternative or supplement to traditional print books. Certain genres in particular have been adopted by digital readers, including science fiction, paranormal fiction, and romance. Many of the greatest rags-to-riches stories in the independent publishing world originated in these niche interest groups and developed a dedicated fan base before spilling into the general market of readers.

Before an e-book can be uploaded and sold, it must be converted from the editable version of a manuscript into a free-flowing file format, typically the open-source ePUB format. This process strips away most of the formatting that dictates how text appears on a page, in order to accommodate the many text customization options featured by e-readers, such as changing the e-book's font size and line spacing to suit reading preferences. Because of this, it's generally wise to have your e-book file conversion done after your manuscript has been heavily edited, as future corrections would have to be applied to both the print version of the book and the digital version individually.

One important decision you need to make as an author publishing digitally is whether to have your print book manually converted into an e-book by a human being or to have the file conversion handled by an automated system. Computer savvy folks can use applications like Calibre, Adobe's InDesign, and Microsoft Word to convert their own text files from the comfort of home; this can be a time-consuming, though reliable method. There are also freelance technicians who will perform this function for a fee, and IngramSpark itself offers this conversion service. Automated conversion systems are cheaper due to the lack of human labor involved, though experience has shown that these systems can be prone to formatting errors (especially the free ones). Do your readers a huge favor—make sure that your e-book is glitch-free and readable before uploading it to the digital market.

The integral role digital publishing has played in the rise of independent publishing has led to heated debate regarding whether such indie books are more likely to attract print readers or digital readers. Naturally, some authors and readers are dedicated to a particular style of reading and rarely deviate from that preference. However, studies have shown that the majority of consistent e-book readers also regularly purchase print books as well. These hybrid readers seem to make buying choices situationally; for instance, an avid reader might enjoy a physical paperback for reading at a park or while relaxing at home, then switch to an e-reader while traveling with limited luggage space or in a dark area (where frontlit screens come in handy).

Consider how your book fits into the situational preferences of your particular audience. Many authors publish their books in a single format only, and while this approach might also work for your book, the prevailing philosophy supports publishing your book in as many different formats as possible, with the goal of making your book accessible to as many different readers as possible.

ACCOUNT SETUP

Once your manuscript has been edited, designed, and otherwise crystallized from raw text and abstract ideas into a set of print-ready PDF files (see page 95), you're ready to experience the full functionality of IngramSpark. As such, you've reached the point in this book where we dive into hands-on publishing, where you'll be required to provide detailed information about yourself and the book you intend to publish. Don't hesitate to consult the glossary at the back of this book if any terms seem foreign, and remember that you can e-mail ingramsparksupport@ ingramcontent.com for assistance if you get stuck at any point.

- Open your web browser.

- In the URL bar, type [www.ingramspark.com]

- Click the "Create New Account" button.

- Click the "Let's Get Started" button.

- Enter your e-mail address, create a password (must be at least eight characters long and must contain at least one letter and one numeral), enter the type of business you represent (e.g. sole proprietorship, S-corporation, C-corporation, nonprofit, etc), enter your mailing information, and click the "Continue" button.

- IngramSpark will prompt you to select and answer a security question, such as "What is the last name of your favorite high school teacher?" and "In what city/town was your first job?" To ensure the safety of your account, IngramSpark will ask this question if there is a need to verify your account should you forget your login or password.

- At this point, IngramSpark will send an e-mail to the address you entered that contains an account activation link; open that e-mail and click the linked text.

- The hyperlink will take you back to IngramSpark's homepage, where you can use the "E-mail Address" and "Password" fields in the top right of the screen to log in to your new IngramSpark account. (Now that you've created your account, you'll access your account this way every time you log in.)

- Read the "Terms of Use" and "Privacy Policy," then click the "I Accept" button.

- IngramSpark will prompt you to review four agreements—the first two are required, while the last two are optional. To confirm each agreement, check the corresponding boxes, enter your full name in the "Signature" field, enter your job title in the "Title" field, then click the "Sign Agreements" button.

  » The Global POD Agreement allows Ingram to produce your titles as print-on-demand books through Ingram's Lightning Source

> **HINT:** If you have provided e-books to Amazon for the Kindle in the past 12 months, Ingram will not be able to provide service to Amazon through the IngramSpark program since you have a previous relationship with Amazon under an existing agreement. If this is the case, do not check "I Accept."

companies in the US, UK, and Australia, as well as the Global Connect and Espresso POD networks.

» The Global E-book Agreement allows Ingram to make your e-book titles available for sale through all of Ingram's e-book distribution partners, apart from Amazon Kindle and Apple (e.g. Kobo and Nook).

» The optional Apple (Agency) E-book Agreement enables your e-books to be distributed to Apple's US and international iBooks and iTunes stores.

» The optional Amazon (Kindle) E-book Addendum enables your e-books to be distributed to Amazon's Kindle platform.

Once you complete these steps, you will have access to your IngramSpark Dashboard, the central hub where you will navigate to each of IngramSpark's many functions (we'll discuss the Dashboard in detail later in this chapter). Before you can add a new title, you must finish adding your publisher compensation information, payment details, and tax information. Ingram needs this data in order to process your payments and remit payments to you for both print-on-demand books and e-books sold to Ingram's retail and library partners. To complete each step, just click the links as shown in the screenshot on page 33.

COMPLETE PUBLISHER COMPENSATION: If you'd prefer to receive your publisher compensation payments through direct deposit to your bank account, merely select the currency used in your country, enter data for your financial institution (your bank's routing number and your bank account number should be inscribed on the bottom of your checks), then click the "Save" button. You also have the option of receiving payments through PayPal; just select the correct currency and provide your PayPal account information. When you're finished, click "Dashboard" on the taskbar to return to the other account setup tasks.

ADD PUBLISHER PAYMENT: IngramSpark users pay for upload fees and print runs using a credit or debit card, saved to their account for convenience. To save a payment card, click the "Add New Card" button, then input your card type, card number, card expiration date, and the mailing address connected with the card. Keep in mind that you may need to return to this page later if your card expires or if you get a new payment card; going forward, you can access your saved payment methods

■ **NOTES:**

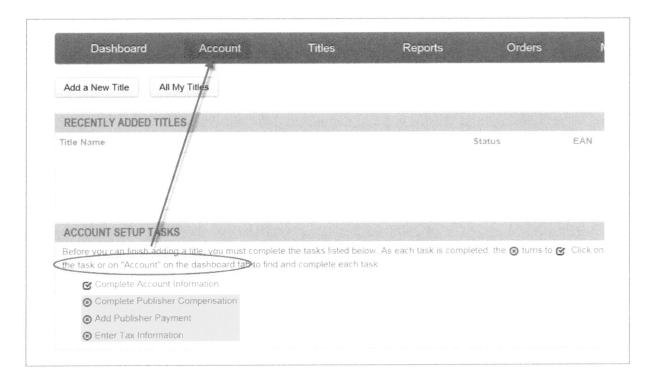

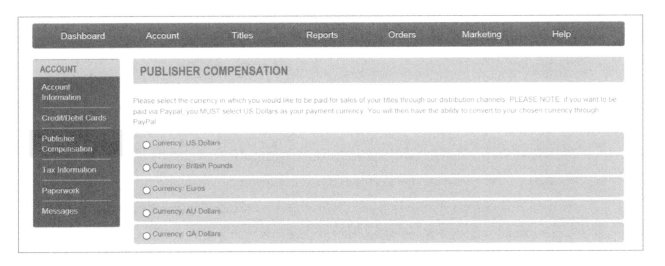

through the "Account" tab of your IngramSpark Dashboard (see diagram on pages 36–37).

ENTER TAX INFORMATION: This step of the process requires you to provide your federal tax-payer ID—this can be your social security number (if you are a sole proprietorship) or your business's employer identification number (if you work for a publishing company). Enter your state, signature, and job title, then click the "Continue" button. If you have a reseller permit or other reason for tax exemption, click the "Claim US Tax Exemptions" button before proceeding to "Continue"—you will then be prompted to provide the necessary documents. Based on the data you provide, IngramSpark will generate a W-9 form for you to review. If you spot any errors, click the "W-9 is not correct" button and fix the data; once all the details are correct, hit the confirmation button. Then you're finished setting up your account!

■ **NOTES:**

HINT: Indie published authors are often responsible for supplying copies of their book to bookstores. Don't want to drive to a distant retailer just to hand deliver books? Save some carbon footprint and have your books shipped directly to the bookstores that sell them. Just be sure someone there is expecting the box to arrive!

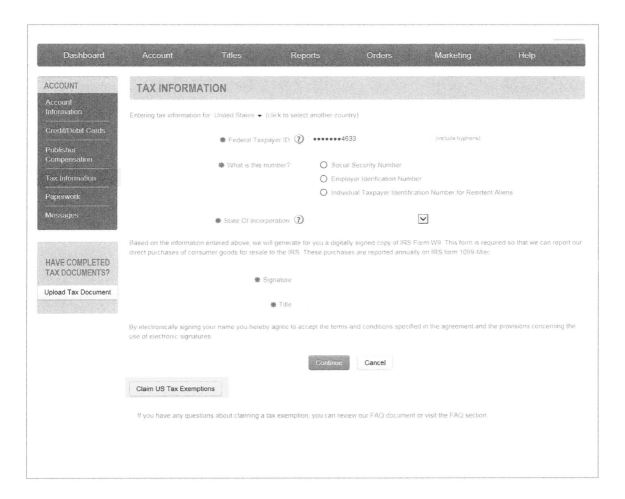

| Dashboard | Account | Titles | Reports | Orders | Marketing | Help |

ACCOUNT

- Account Information
- Credit/Debit Cards
- Publisher Compensation
- Tax Information
- Paperwork
- Messages

HAVE COMPLETED TAX DOCUMENTS?

Upload Tax Document

TAX INFORMATION

Entering tax information for United States ▼ (click to select another country)

✱ Federal Taxpayer ID: (?) •••••••4633   (include hyphens)

✱ What is this number?   ○ Social Security Number

○ Employer Idenfication Number

○ Individual Taxpayer Identification Number for Resident Aliens

✱ State Of Incorporation: (?)   ☑

Based on the information entered above, we will generate for you a digitally signed copy of IRS Form W9. This form is required so that we can report our direct purchases of consumer goods for resale to the IRS. These purchases are reported annually on IRS form 1099-Misc

✱ Signature

✱ Title

By electronically signing your name you hereby agree to accept the terms and conditions specified in the agreement and the provisions concerning the use of electronic signatures.

Continue   Cancel

Claim US Tax Exemptions

If you have any questions about claiming a tax exemption, you can review our FAQ document or visit the FAQ section.

the IngramSpark Dashboard

ACCOUNT: This tab gives you access to your basic account information, your saved payment methods, your tax status, and copies of the agreements you signed in account setup.

DASHBOARD: Click this tab from elsewhere on the site to return to your Dashboard.

IngramSpark℠

| Dashboard | Account | Titles |

ADD A NEW TITLE: Turn the page to the next chapter and discover how to upload your book to IngramSpark!

Add a New Title   All My Titles

RECENTLY ADDED TITLES

Title Name   Status

TITLES: This tab contains a list of every individual title you've uploaded to IngramSpark, which can be sorted by title, author, ISBN, binding format, status, or date originally uploaded. You can also add new titles from this tab, access digital proofs that require your approval, and promote your titles through Ingram's marketing channel (more on this in the "Marketing" chapter).

REPORTS: Click here to generate reports covering e-book sales, print book sales, bills you've received from Ingram, invoices, and a record of all transactions made through your IngramSpark account (more on this in the "Orders and Reports" chapter).

CONTACT US: This button directs you to Ingram's support team, who can be reached by phone or e-mail.

MESSAGES: This is your IngramSpark inbox, where IngramSpark alerts you to site maintenance and proofs that require your attention. You typically will be notified of issues with your titles directly by e-mail.

ACCOUNT #: This is the reference number associated with your account. It's a good idea to include this number in the subject line any time you e-mail customer support.

Welcome Back Customer Name
IngramSpark Account 9000012

(Sign out)

Contact Us

3   You have unread messages.

Reports	Orders	Marketing	Help

AN	Format	Author	Action

HELP: Many of IngramSpark's most useful functions are compiled under this tab. Click the "Tools" link on the left side of the screen to access the Cover Template Generator, along with calculators that determine print & shipping costs, publisher's compensation, book weight, and spine width, based on the metadata you enter.

ORDERS: Use this handy tab to order print copies in any quantity you require, from a single copy to thousands of books. Since you must select an address for your bound books to be shipped to when you order them, your previous shipping addresses are saved here as well.

MARKETING: This tab gives you access to Ingram's marketing channels (more on this in the "Marketing" chapter).

TITLE UPLOAD

Click the "Add a New Title" button on your Dashboard or under the "Titles" tab to begin the upload process. Be prepared to provide concrete details on the specific features and dimensions of your book. Ingram needs to know a lot about your book in order to distribute it effectively, and this chapter covers much of that information in detail. Don't stress about it too much though; you can come back and change your book's metadata at any time.

> **HINT:** If you haven't decided on certain details like list price or physical dimensions, visit a bookstore and find the section where your book would be shelved. You can learn a lot by observing the books that your book will be rubbing shoulders with, including popular binding sizes, what to include on your cover, and the average price readers expect to pay for the type of book you've written. If you can price your book for slightly less than other books in its genre, your book may have a competitive edge when potential buyers try to decide between your book and another.

Basic Metadata

The first distinction you must make is whether your title will be published in print, in digital, or both. IngramSpark charges a $49 upload fee for titles published in print and a $25 upload fee for titles published as e-books. However, if you upload both the print and digital versions at the same time, the total fee for both uploads is only $49. Furthermore, IngramSpark will issue you a $49 credit if you order a print run of 50 books or more within 60 days after uploading the title. Select one of the three options under "Select Product Type," then proceed to the following fields.

TITLE: The main title of your book. Do not include a subtitle here.

SUBTITLE: Flavor text attached to the end of the main title. This can be a more precise description of your book's subject matter, or simply "A Novel," or "Volume IV," or nothing at all. This field can be left blank if your book has no subtitle.

LANGUAGE: The language your book is written in.

SHORT DESCRIPTION: A very brief summary of your book's content. Think of this as an elevator pitch (i.e. a descriptive mini-speech introducing someone to your book, which should be quick enough to

Step 1 of 7 - Basic Metadata

deliver while riding an elevator). Once you've written it down, practice it out loud so you've got it memorized the next time you're in an elevator!

KEYWORDS: Enter 4-8 words that explicitly reflect the content of your book (e.g. memoir, paranormal, Renaissance, bildungsroman, etc). These keywords will help your book appear in online searches made by customers browsing by subject.

SERIES NAME AND NUMBER: If your book is part of a series, enter the name of the series here to link all titles in that series together. Then enter the correct number of the book you're uploading, to keep your titles in the correct order. Some series have unique names (e.g. the His Dark Materials trilogy), while others are simply named after the first book (e.g. the Redwall series), or named after the main protagonist (e.g. the Harry Hole novels).

EDITION DESCRIPTION: For your first time uploading any given title, enter "1st edition" in this field. If your book undergoes a significant revision or if you add a chapter or more of new content (enough to warrant assigning the new version a unique ISBN), the new version should be marked "2nd edition," and so on.

DESCRIPTION: In this space, copy and paste the primary marketing blurb from the back cover of

Select Product Type

- ◉ Print and Ebook — *Ready to submit interior and cover files in both formats*
- ○ Print Only — *Ready to submit a PDF interior and a PDF cover file.*
- ○ Ebook Only — *Ready to submit an EPUB interior and a JPG cover file.*

Key

- ✳ Required Fields
- ⑦ Help Text
- ⊗ Validation Error

ABOUT YOUR BOOK

✳ Title ⑦   IngramSpark Guide to Independent Publishing

Subtitle

✳ Language ⑦   English ▾

Short Description ⑦
Max 350 characters

Keywords ⑦   Ingram, IngramSpark, independent publishing, self published author
(separated by commas)

Series Name and   #
Number ⑦

Edition Description ⑦

✳ Full Description ⑦   **B** *I* U S x₂ x² ⚭ ⚭ ▐   ≔ ≔ ⊣≣ ⊣≣ 99 ⟨⟩ Source
Min 200 to Max 4000
characters

The *IngramSpark Guide to Independent Publishing* is essential for publishers wanting

Step 1 of 7 - Basic Metadata cont'd

your book. Also, feel free to use bolds, italics, and other formatting in this field. You're required to fill this space with at least 200 characters before you can continue—if you have no description prepared, you could simply fill the space with 200 zeros to skip this step for the time being.

Click the "Continue to Step 2 of 7"
button to continue.

CONTRIBUTORS: Enter the last name of the author here first. Then add the author's first name and middle initial (optional). Take note that this is the name that will be publically listed as the author of your book in Ingram's database and distribution network; so, if you write under a pen name, pseudonym, or nom de plume, now is the time to lock it in. If your book credits an illustrator or editor alongside the author, enter his or her name as well, then choose the appropriate job title from the dropdown menu on the right-hand side of the screen. Click the "About Contributor . . . " button next to any contributor to provide additional information about that contributor.

BIOGRAPHY: A quick and tidy summary of each contributor's identity. In the case of the author, this can be copy/pasted from the author bio on the back cover of your book. If you're stuck writing a bio, pick up a few books from a nearby shelf and read the bios for those authors for inspiration; the

■ NOTES:

Select Product Type		Key	
⦿ Print and Ebook	*Ready to submit interior and cover files in both formats.*	✱	Required Fields
○ Print Only	*Ready to submit a PDF interior and a PDF cover file.*	⑦	Help Text
○ Ebook Only	*Ready to submit an EPUB interior and a JPG cover file.*	⊗	Validation Error

ABOUT THE AUTHOR/CONTRIBUTORS

✱ Contributors ⑦

	Last Name	First Name	Middle	Role	
✱ 1:	Clark	Brendan		Author ▾	About Contributor...

Biography ⑦

Prior Work ⑦

Location ⑦

Affiliations ⑦

Step 2 of 7

trick is to be brief, while also communicating something unique and interesting about yourself.

PRIOR WORK: Here you can list other titles you've published or collaborated on. This can help consumers discover new books by you if they read one of your books and enjoyed it enough to look it up online.

LOCATION: Enter your location here if you identify with a particular area. This can attract readers searching for authors in their own local community.

AFFILIATIONS: Here you can list any organizations, agencies, schools, or nonprofits you're associated with.

Click the "Continue to Step 3 of 7" button
to move forward.

IMPRINT: The particular house that publishes a book is often a subsidiary (known in the book industry as an "imprint") of a larger publishing house. By default, your imprint will be listed by IngramSpark as the business name associated with your account; you can also request an additional imprint name by clicking the link.

SUBJECTS: Rather than typing into the space provided here, click the "Find Subjects" button. This

■ **NOTES:**

CATEGORIZE YOUR BOOK

✱ Imprint (?)   **Graphic Arts Publications**   ☑   Request another imprint (?)

✱ Subjects (?)

       ✱ 1:   [Find Subjects]   LAN027000   Language Arts & Disciplines : Publishir

         2:   [Find Subjects]

         3:   [Find Subjects]

Regional Subject (?)   [   ]   [Find Regions]

✱ Audience (?)   Trade/General (Adult)   ☑

Table of Contents (?)

Review Quotes (?)

Does your book have   ○ Yes   ○ No
photographs and/or
illustrations?

Step 3 of 7

will open a new window with a search bar; type into that search bar a very simple classification for your book (e.g. fiction, science, biography, history, dogs, crafts, etc). The keyword you enter will generate a list of possible genres, which you can choose by clicking the square next to the appropriate classification. If you don't see anything that accurately describes your book, feel free to try another keyword; it's normal to try a few times for more obscure genres. You can apply up to three subject classifications to your book, though you're only required to choose one. The more subject codes you apply to your title, the more frequently it will appear in the search results of customers searching for similar books online.

REGIONAL SUBJECT: If your book takes place in a particular region of the world (e.g. Pacific Northwest US, South Australia) you can search for that locality by clicking the "Find Regions" button.

AUDIENCE: Identify your title as a textbook, children's book, young adult book, adult/general book, or scholarly/professional book. If your book is not marketed to a particular age range, it's best to default to adult/general.

TABLE OF CONTENTS: Here you can copy/paste your table of contents to provide a list of all chapters included in your book. This is generally unnecessary for fiction, but for nonfiction it can be very helpful for readers to see exactly what kind of information they can acquire by reading your book.

REVIEW QUOTES: Use this field to enter quotations from people who have favorably reviewed your book (and given you permission to publicize their words). For recommendations longer than a couple sentences, it's best to provide a brief excerpt rather than the full text.

ILLUSTRATIONS/PHOTOGRAPHS: Confirm whether your book contains images or not. If you select "Yes," you'll be prompted to specify whether your images are black & white or color, and how many there are total.

Click the "Continue to Step 4 of 7" button
to move forward.

TRIM SIZE: Choose the appropriate physical dimensions for your book from the drop-down menu (see list of possible dimensions on page 12). Popular sizes for trade paperbacks are 5x8, 6x9, and 7x10, while 8x8 is very popular for kid's picture books. You should make your decision based on what you think would be the best fit for your book.

INTERIOR COLOR AND PAPER: Next, select whether your book should be printed in black & white (i.e. printed with toner) or in full color (i.e. printed with ink). For black & white books, you can choose between cream and white paper. IngramSpark offers two levels of color print quality, standard color and premium color. Standard color is suitable for most books where you just need spot color, although more and more children's authors are making this choice because of the price: it is roughly a third of the cost of the premium color option. Premium is a good choice for coffee table–type books or where color is more critical.

BINDING TYPE: Specify whether the book you're uploading should be printed as a paperback or a hardcover. Paperbacks can be either perfect bound (i.e. bound with hot glue applied to the spine) or saddle stitched (i.e. held together with staples applied to the spine); hardcovers can be either case bound (i.e. bound with the cover image printed directly onto a rigid cover) or cloth bound (i.e. bound to a rigid cover coated in fabric). Cloth bound books can be produced with either gray or blue fabric, either with or without a dust jacket. Depending on which trim size you selected earlier, some binding types may be unavailable; for example, IngramSpark cannot produce a 7x10 book as a cloth bound hardcover, only as a paperback or case bound hardcover (see the tables on pages 52–53 for more information on which binding types are compatible with certain trim sizes).

LAMINATE TYPE: IngramSpark offers two varieties of cover laminate; gloss covers are reflective and enhance vibrant colors, while matte covers feature a muted finish that softens colors and makes type-heavy covers easier to read. Again, this choice mainly boils down to the particular style of your book and your own personal taste.

STAMPED TEXT: These spaces only appear when "cloth bound" has been selected under "Binding Type." As part of the production process, these books can have the title, author name, or other text embossed in golden letters along the spine of the fabric-coated cover. You can enter text in any of the three spaces, depending on how you want the text oriented on the spine (for example, you could enter the title of your book in the "Left Justified" space and your name in the "Right Justified" space, or just enter the title in the "Centered" space).

■ **NOTES:**

HINT: If you're undecided between cream and white paper, consider which more accurately suits the tone of your book. The general view is that cream paper makes a book seem more personal and informal, while white paper conveys a more academic and professional effect. You can also judge based on which paper type more comfortably matches the colors used on your book's cover.

PRINT FORMAT

Click on "Help" in the top menu to estimate print and shipping costs and to use our cover creator tool (highly recommended).

✳ Trim Size ⑦   6.000" x 9.000" (229mm x 152mm) ▼

Interior Color and Paper ⑦ ◉ Black & White
- ◉ White   B&W printed on 50lb White paper
- ◯ Creme   B&W printed on 50lb Creme paper
- ◯ Color

Binding Type ⑦ ◉ Paperback
- ◉ Perfect Bound   Glued spine with color laminated cover
- ◯ Saddle Stitch   Stapled pages with color laminated cover, 4-48 page count
- ◯ Hardback

Laminate Type ⑦
- ◯ Cloth(None)
- ◯ Gloss
- ◉ Matte

✳ Page Count ⑦   150

Step 4 of 7

TRIM SIZE MATRIX

Note: blank white cells indicate not available

			B&W		Standard/Select Color			Premium Color
Product and Paper Types			50lb/80gsm Creme	50lb/75gsm White	50lb/75gsm White	45lb/66gsm White	70lb/105gsm White	70lb/105gsm White
Page Range			18-1050 pgs	18-1200 pgs	18-1200 pgs	24-1200 pgs	18-900 pgs (PF) / 18-840 pgs (HC)	24-900 pgs(PF) / 24-840 pgs(HC) / 4-48 pgs(SS)
inches	mm	Bindtype	☐ B&W Available		☐ Standard/Select Color Available			☐ Premium Color Available
4 x 6	152 x 102	Perfectbound						
4 x 7	178 x 102	Perfectbound						
4.25 x 7	178 x 108	Perfectbound						
4.37 x 7	178 x 111	Perfectbound						
4.72 x 7.48	190 x 120	Perfectbound						
5 x 7	178 x 127	Perfectbound						
5 x 8	203 x 127	Perfectbound / Case Laminate / Cloth (Blue) / Cloth (Gray) / Jacketed (Blue Cloth) / Jacketed (Gray Cloth)						
5.06 x 7.81	198 x 129	Perfectbound						
5.25 x 8	203 x 133	Perfectbound						
5.5 x 8.25	210 x 140	Perfectbound						
5.5 X 8.5 (Demy 8vo)	216 X 140	Perfectbound / Case Laminate / Cloth (Blue) / Cloth (Gray) / Jacketed (Blue Cloth) / Jacketed (Gray Cloth) / Saddle Stitch						
5.83 x 8.27 (A5)	210 X 148	Perfectbound						
6 x 9	229 x 152	Perfectbound / Case Laminate / Cloth (Blue) / Cloth (Gray) / Jacketed (Blue Cloth) / Jacketed (Gray Cloth) / Saddle Stitch						
6.14 x 9.21 (Royal 8vo)	234 x 156	Perfectbound / Case Laminate / Cloth (Blue) / Cloth (Gray) / Jacketed (Blue Cloth) / Jacketed (Gray Cloth) / Saddle Stitch						
6.625 x 10.25	260 x 168	Perfectbound / Saddle Stitch						
6.69 x 9.61 (pinched crown)	244 x 170	Perfectbound / Case Laminate						
7 x 10	254 x 178	Perfectbound / Case Laminate / Saddle Stitch						
7.44 x 9.69 (crown 4vo)	246 x 189	Perfectbound						
7.50 x 9.25	235 x 191	Perfectbound / Case Laminate / Saddle Stitch						
8 x 8	203 x 203	Perfectbound / Case Laminate / Saddle Stitch						
8 x 10	254 x 203	Perfectbound / Case Laminate / Saddle Stitch						

TRIM SIZES

GLOSS or MATTE lamination

Perforation Available for Standard Color Perfectbound 50lb/75gsm Sizes: 6 x 9, 7.5 x 9.25, 8 x 10, 8.5 x 11

TRIM SIZE MATRIX

Product and Paper Types		B&W		Standard/Select Color			Premium Color
		50lb/80gsm Creme	50lb/75gsm White	50lb/75gsm White	45lb/66gsm White	70lb/105gsm White	70lb/105gsm White
Page Range		18-1050 pgs	18-1200 pgs	18-1200 pgs	24-1200 pgs	18-900 pgs (PF) 18-840 pgs (HC)	24-900 pgs(PF) 24-840 pgs(HC) 4-48 pgs(SS)
inches	mm	Bindtype	☐ B&W Available		☐ Standard/Select Color Available		☐ Premium Color Available
8 x 10.88	276 x 203	Perfectbound					
		Case Laminate					
8.25 x 10.75	273 x 210	Perfectbound					
		Case Laminate					
		Saddle Stitch					
8.25 x 11	280 x 210	Perfectbound					
8.268 x 11.693 (A4)	297 x 210	Perfectbound					
8.5 x 8.5	216 x 216	Perfectbound					
		Case Laminate					
		Saddle Stitch					
8.5 x 9	229 x 216	Perfectbound					
8.5 x 11	280 x 216	Perfectbound					
		Case Laminate					
		Saddle Stitch					

GLOSS or MATTE lamination

Perforation Available for Standard Color Perfectbound 50lb/75gsm Sizes: 6 x 9, 7.5 x 9.25, 8 x 10, 8.5 x 11

DUPLEX COVERS MATRIX

Note: blank white cells indicate not available

Product and Paper Types		B&W		Standard/Select Color			Premium Color
		50lb/80gsm Creme	50lb/75gsm White	50lb/75gsm White	45lb/66gsm White	70lb/105gsm White	70lb/105gsm White
Page Ranges			min 18 pgs- (max below)	min 18 pgs- (max below)	min 24 pgs- (max below)	min 18 pgs- (max below)	min 24 pgs- (max below)
inches	mm	Bindtype	☐ B&W Available		☐ Standard/Select Color Available		☐ Premium Color Available
6.625 x 10.25	260 x 168	Perfectbound		1200	1200	1200	900	900
6.69 x 9.61 (pinched crown)	244 x 170	Perfectbound		1200	1200	1200	900	900
7 x 10	254 x 178	Perfectbound		1140	1140	1200	740	740
7.44 x 9.69 (crown 4vo)	246 x 189	Perfectbound		900	900	1020	640	
7.50 x 9.25	235 x 191	Perfectbound		840	840	1020	640	640
8 x 8	203 x 203	Perfectbound		580	580	700	440	440
8 x 10	254 x 203	Perfectbound		580	580	700	440	440
8 x 10.88	276 x 203	Perfectbound		580	580	700	440	440
8.25 x 10.75	273 x 210	Perfectbound		500	500	540	340	340
8.25 x 11	280 x 210	Perfectbound		500	500	540	340	
8.5 x 8.5	216 x 216	Perfectbound		240	240	280	180	180
8.5 x 9	229 x 216	Perfectbound		240	240	280	180	180
8.5 x 11	280 x 216	Perfectbound		240	240	280	180	180

GLOSS or MATTE lamination

Perforation Available for Standard Color Perfectbound 50lb/75gsm Sizes: 7.5 x 9.25, 8 x 10, 8.5 x 11

PAGE COUNT: Enter the number of individual pages in your book (including all the blank pages)—one sheet of paper, back and front, counts as two book pages. Your final page count must be an even number equal to or greater than 18 pages and lower than 1,200 pages. Bear in mind that IngramSpark adds an additional left-hand page to the end of your page block for the printer's barcode that provides information as to where the book was printed, so if the last page of your book's interior is a right-hand page, IngramSpark will add one page to the total page count, and if the last page of your book's interior is a left-hand page, IngramSpark will add two pages to the total page count.

■ **NOTES:**

HINT: This page is where you determine conditions for selling your book through Ingram's extended distribution network. Once your title has been enabled for distribution, it will become discoverable on Ingram's digital inventory, which is used by book retailers to stock their shelves and fulfill orders for customers. Here's how the process works—a customer walks into a bookstore (or visits the retailer's website) and asks for your book; the retailer finds your book listed in Ingram's inventory and places an order for it; a single copy of your book is printed-on-demand at Ingram's bindery and shipped to the retailer, typically within 5–7 days; the happy customer then pays for the book and takes it home.

Click the "Continue to Step 5 of 7" button
to move forward.

PRINT ISBN: Enter your book's ISBN here. An ISBN (International Standard Book Number), also known as EAN (European Article Number), is a unique thirteen-digit item code provided by your country's ISBN agency and assigned by publishers to identify the particular format and edition of a particular title. So, a traditionally published book will usually have three different ISBNs—one for the hardcover edition, one for the paperback edition, and one for the digital edition. Indie published authors in the US are responsible for acquiring ISBNs for their books by purchasing them from Bowker, the US ISBN Agency (www.myidentifiers.com); you can also purchase ISBNs through IngramSpark for $85 each by selecting "Click here if you would like to purchase an ISBN (an ISBN is required for distribution)". Bowker sells a single ISBN for $125, 10 ISBNs for $295, or 100 ISBNs for $575; therefore, it's always advisable to purchase ISBNs in bulk, unless you are certain that you will use only one ISBN for the entirety of your publishing career. Retailers and distributors often require that indie published titles have an ISBN assigned to them for sales and inventory purposes. That said, IngramSpark can assign a free custom item code to your book for printing purposes if you do not intend to distribute your book through Ingram; just select "Click here if you would like a non-distributable SKU to be assigned to this title." Finally, be sure to use the same ISBN for your book on all sales channels. Listing the same book with different ISBNs on multiple distributors may confuse retailers trying to purchase your book. Note that publishers from countries outside of the US should research where to obtain an ISBN specific for your country. In many countries, such as Canada, ISBNs are provided for free by the government but it varies from country to country.

PRICING: Use this grid to determine the price readers will pay for your book, the cut that will be kept by the retailer who sells your book, and the profit you will receive from print-on-demand sales through Ingram's distribution channel.

PRINT FORMAT

❋ Print ISBN ⑦   [978-1476727653]   Click here if you would like to purchase an ISBN (an ISBN is required for distribution)

Click here if you would like a non-distributable SKU to be assigned to this title

PRICING

For your content to be available for sale in each market below, you must provide the Print Retail Price, wholesale discount and returnable option. To assist with converting currency you can access the Currency Converter.

Market ⑦	Print Retail Price ⑦	Wholesale Discount ⑦	Returnable ⑦	Compensation
United States	US$ [9.99]	55% trade (retailer preference) ▾	Yes - Delive ▾	US$ 1.65
United Kingdom	£ [6.50]	55% trade (retailer preference) ▾	No ▾	£ 0.72
European Union	€ [9.00]	55% trade (retailer preference) ▾	No ▾	€ 1.6
Canada	CA$ [13.20]	55% trade (retailer preference) ▾	No ▾	
Australia	AU$ [13.20]	55% trade (retailer preference) ▾	No ▾	AU$ 1.64

○ Copy United States Print Retail Price and Wholesale Discount to the Global Connect Program

| Global Connect Program ⑦ | US$ [9.99] | 55% trade (retailer preference) ▾ | No ▾ | US$ 1.65 |

❋ Publication Date ⑦   [9/15/2015]   🗓

On Sale Date ⑦   [9/30/2015]   🗓

Step 5 of 7

- **Market:** You can assign different list prices to your title for each region where you plan to sell your book. These regional markets include the United States (price in US dollars), the United Kingdom (price in pounds), the European Union (price in Euros), Canada (price in Canadian dollars), and Australia (price in Australian dollars). Other regions of the world get books through Ingram's Global Connect Program (represented at the bottom of the grid), using a price in US dollars. You are not required to make your book available in all markets, and you do so by filling in the market pricing; so, if you don't want to make your book available for sale in Canada, just skip the Canadian pricing.

- **Print Retail Price:** This is the price that retailers will charge their customers when selling your book (retailers may offer discounts to customers for promotions or coupons, but those are taken out of the retailer's profit, not yours). Though you're not required to display your book's list price on the back cover of your book, doing so adds a level of professionalism to the visual appearance of your book. I recommend assigning a price to your title that conforms to trade standard pricing, i.e. ending in 95 cents, 99 cents, or an even dollar amount.

- **Wholesale Discount:** If a product's retail price is the amount of money a consumer pays when he or she purchases the product, that product's wholesale price is the amount of money that a retailer pays the product's manufacturer to acquire the product. For our purposes, the wholesale discount applied to your book is essentially the portion of your book's retail price that is kept by both the retailer (bookstores) and the distributor (Ingram) combined. Ingram keeps 10–15% as a distribution fee by default, so the trade standard wholesale discount of 55% can be roughly broken down into 15% for Ingram and 40% for the retailer. I highly recommend using trade standard wholesale terms, as many retailers will refuse to stock a book on their shelves if the wholesale discount is below a certain threshold; typically, retailers will only order a short-discount title (less than 35%)

if a customer specifically requests it, and the retailer will often charge the customer an extra fee to make up for the meager profit they would otherwise make from the sale. However, if you decide to assign a lower wholesale discount, just select "Other" from the drop-down menu and enter a discount percentage.

Returnable: Bookstores typically have the option of returning unsold merchandise to the publisher after a certain amount of time on the shelf. You have three options here:

> » **Yes – Deliver:** Returned books will be shipped to the default mailing address on your IngramSpark account. You will be billed for the profit you made on the original sale of that book, plus the cost of shipping the book.

> » **Yes – Destroy:** Returned books will be reduced to pulp. You will be billed for the profit you made on the original sale of that book.

> » **No:** Retailers will not be allowed to return copies of this title, and because of this are extremely unlikely to stock your book in their inventory except in the event of special orders from customers.

Compensation: This auto-generated amount represents the profit you would make from each print-on-demand sale of this title through Ingram to retail or library partners. (Units that you order and sell directly are not factored into compensation.) You are compensated based on the retail price and wholesale discount you entered when you set up your title. This is calculated as: list price – (wholesale discount x list price) – printing cost = publisher's compensation. So (hypothetically), if a book were priced at $15, had a printing cost of $3.20, and was set to a trade standard wholesale discount (55%), the equation would look like this: $15 – (55% translates to $8.25) – $3.20 =

HINT: If you're trying to decide how much you should price your book for, try experimenting with a few different price points to see which strikes the right balance between profitability and competitiveness. Just set the wholesale discount you've decided on, input a price, and see what IngramSpark calculates as your publisher's compensation. If the pub comp is a negative number, you know you need to aim for a higher price point. Once the pub comp climbs above zero, you know you've found your minimum list price. If you want to make more profit per sale, increase the list price. Be aware that extravagantly expensive books can deter potential buyers; it's often more profitable long-term to make a bit less money for each sale and encourage a higher volume of sales with a more competitive price. Again, I highly recommend using the prices of published books similar to your book as examples when determining your own price point.

$3.55 publisher compensation/unit. Typically, Ingram remits these payments within 90 days of the month-end reporting period following the sale.

PUBLICATION DATE: This is the official release date of your book. New books are typically released on Tuesdays. Be sure to make this date far enough in the future that you will have time to order a bound proof, apply any revisions that arise from the proofing process, and have your first print run produced at least a month before your publication date. Publishing a book can be a chaotic process, and should any unexpected delays occur, a cushion of extra time will be your best friend.

ON SALE DATE: This is the date upon which retailers are allowed to sell your book. You can set this date to before your title's publication date to allow prepublication sales, or after your title's publication date in the event that you need to issue an emergency reprint.

Click the "Continue to Step 6 of 7" button
to move forward.

E-BOOK ISBN: Since the digital edition of a book requires its own ISBN, you'll need to provide an additional ISBN here when you upload your e-book.

PRICING: Again, enter a list price for your e-book for each regional market you want to make your book available to. Take note that while the "E-book Retail Price" can be any numeric amount with two decimal places, the "Apple E-book (Agency) Price" must end in 99 cents (e.g. $3.99, $9.99, $0.99). Most e-book platforms price their books according to the "E-book Retail Price," but e-books sold through Apple's iTunes Store follow the "Apple E-book (Agency) Price"; furthermore, some e-book retailers will assign

■ **NOTES:**

HINT: The e-book version of a book typically has a list price close to 60% of the current print edition, usually ending in 99 cents.

EBOOK FORMAT

✳ Ebook ISBN (?)   978-1781162644   Click here if you would like to purchase an ISBN (an ISBN is required for distribution)

PRICING

Currencies (?)	Ebook Retail Price (?)	Apple Ebook (Agency) Price (?)	Compensation
US Dollars	US$ 4.00	US$ 3.99	US$ 1.60
British Pounds	£ 5.00	£ 4.99	£ 2.00
Euros	€ 5.00	€ 4.99	€ 2.00
CA Dollars	CA$ 5.00	CA$ 4.99	CA$ 2.00
AU Dollars	AU$ 5.00	AU$ 4.99	AU$ 2.00

✳ Publication Date (?)   10/15/2015

✳ On Sale Date (?)   10/31/2015

✳ Page Count (?)   100

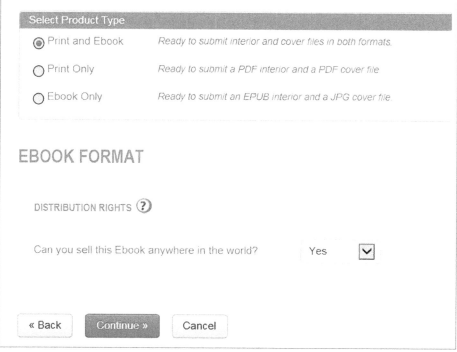

Select Product Type

🔘 Print and Ebook   *Ready to submit interior and cover files in both formats.*

⭕ Print Only   *Ready to submit a PDF interior and a PDF cover file*

⭕ Ebook Only   *Ready to submit an EPUB interior and a JPG cover file.*

EBOOK FORMAT

DISTRIBUTION RIGHTS (?)

Can you sell this Ebook anywhere in the world?   Yes ▾

« Back   Continue »   Cancel

Step 6 of 7 (top), 7 of 7 (bottom)

their own price to your e-book, but regardless of the price they use they must still pay you the amount listed in "Compensation." This is a big benefit to using IngramSpark since your profits aren't reduced if the retailer lowers the price on their site.

Reenter your publication date, on sale date, and page count, then click the "Continue to Step 7 of 7" button to move forward.

DISTRIBUTION RIGHTS: If you own the rights to sell this digital content anywhere in the world, select "Yes." This should be true if you are the author of the e-book you're uploading, but research your regional copyright laws if you feel unsure. If you select "No," you will be presented with a list of regional markets to go through and check or uncheck. IngramSpark will also encourage you (as do I) to contact your customer support team if you need any help completing this step.

Click the "Continue" button to move forward.

On this page you must upload a total of four files (two if you are uploading only the print edition or only the digital edition); these files constitute the full content of your book, including both page block and cover spread.

■ NOTES:

TITLE FILES

INGRAMSPARK GUIDE TO INDEPENDENT PUBLISHING

PRINT

ISBN/SKU:	9781476727653
ISBN Complete:	978-1476727653
Publication Date:	9/15/2015
Street Date:	9/30/2015

BOOK TYPE

B&W 6 x 9 in or 229 x 152 mm Perfect Bound on White w/Matte Lam

INTERIOR FILE

9780495801924_txt.pdf
Uploaded: 9/17/2013 12:05:25 PM
DRAG & DROP REPLACEMENT INTERIOR PDF HERE
or
SELECT TO UPLOAD
Browse

COVER FILE

9781480167315_cover.pdf
Uploaded: 9/17/2013 12:07:07 PM
DRAG & DROP REPLACEMENT COVER PDF HERE
or
SELECT TO UPLOAD
Browse

EBOOK

ISBN/SKU:	9781781162644
ISBN Complete:	978-1781162644
Publication Date:	10/15/2015
Street Date:	10/31/2015

BOOK TYPE

Adobe eBook ePub

EBOOK FILE

9781935993063_EPUB.epub
Uploaded: 9/17/2013 12:07:39 PM
DRAG & DROP REPLACEMENT EPUB HERE
or
SELECT TO UPLOAD
Browse

COVER IMAGE FILE

9781938736018_FC.jpg
Uploaded: 9/17/2013 12:07:51 PM
DRAG & DROP REPLACEMENT COVER JPG HERE
or
SELECT TO UPLOAD
Browse

When all files are uploaded, hit continue. Files will go through step one of a two step validation process. If there are errors, you will be alerted on the next screen.

« Back   Cancel   Continue »

Upload page

Print Interior File

This PDF file must include the full text of your book in single pages (not two-page reader's spreads), formatted from the very first page to the very last page with the margins, fonts, and page dimensions of the finished book. What you see on each page of the PDF is what you'll see on each page of your bound book, so be sure that it is truly print-ready before you order a massive quantity of books. To upload the file, simply open the folder containing your interior PDF file and drag it into the box marked "Interior File"; you can also use the "Browse" button in that box to locate the file from within your computer.

Print Cover File

To upload cover art for your book, you must super-impose the full cover spread on a template

HINT: If you've hired a freelance graphic designer to create your cover spread, enter their e-mail address instead of your own. Then, simply ask your designer to place your cover art directly onto the template and return the combined file to you as a PDF. This will also allow them to visually check that the proportions of your cover spread fit the spatial requirements of the template.

COVER TEMPLATE GENERATOR

Once you complete and submit the data below, we will email you back a template and support files to be used to build your cover.

Included in the email will be instructions for using the template, creating an appropriate PostScript file and distilling a PDF to our specifications.

✱ 13 Digit ISBN

Publisher Reference Number

✱ Trim Size [▼]

Interior Color and Paper ⑦   ○ Black & White
○ Color

Binding Type ⑦   ○ Paperback
○ Hardback

Laminate Type ⑦   ○ Gloss
○ Matte

✱ Page Count

✱ File Type   InDesign CS3 and newer [▼]

✱ Email Address

✱ Confirm Email Address

OPTIONAL INFORMATION

Price

Currency   US Dollars [▼]

Price in Bar Code   No [▼]

[Submit]

generated by IngramSpark. To download one of these templates, click the "Help" tab from the taskbar near the top of your screen and select "Cover Template Generator." IngramSpark will then prompt you to enter some basic metadata for your book; if you've followed me throughout this chapter you need only enter your ISBN and IngramSpark will auto-populate the rest of the data. Then, select the template file format you prefer from the drop-down menu—InDesign, EPS, or PDF (personally, I always use PDF)—and enter your e-mail address.

These templates come with a complementary barcode encoded with your title's ISBN. If you want to add pricing details to that barcode, enter your book's list price,

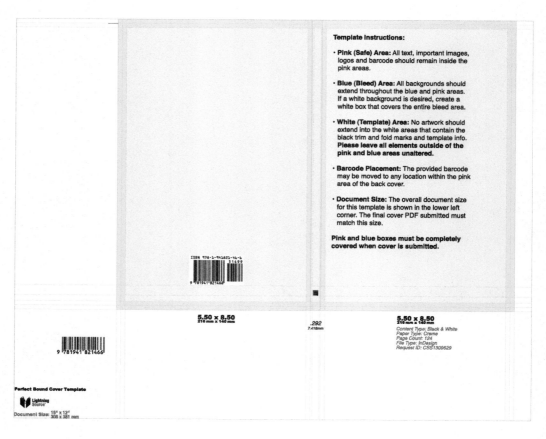

Typical softbound cover template showing the pink "active" areas and the blue "safety" areas.

> **HINT:** It's highly recommended that you save both print files in PDF/X-1a format. If you're not sure how to do that, upload regular PDF files—IngramSpark's customer support team will alert you to any technical problems with your files and render assistance as needed with fixing the issue.

select your regional currency, and select "Yes" from the drop-down menu. Once you click the "Submit" button, IngramSpark will generate your template and send it to you as an e-mail attachment.

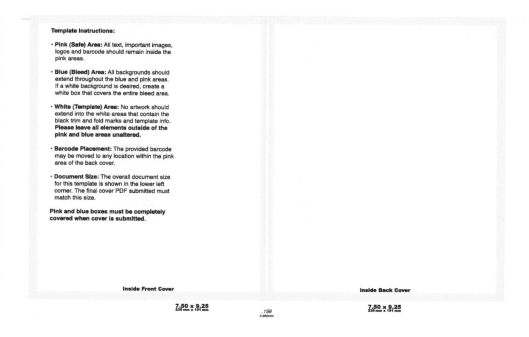

Inside printed duplex cover for a softbound book.

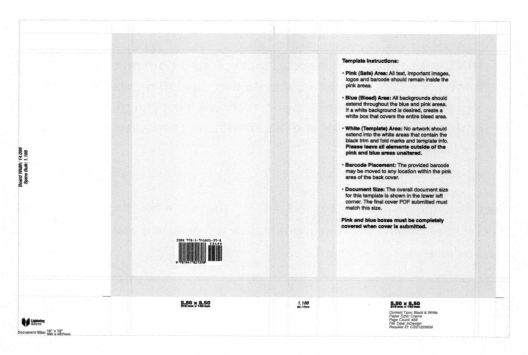

Cover template for a casebound book.

Cover template for a saddle stitched book.
Note the difference in setup around the spine area.

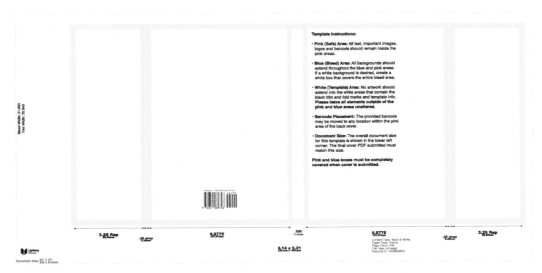

A dust jacket template for a clothbound book.

Download and open the attached PDF; once you've done so, you'll see that your cover art must fit over color-coded spaces. The pink areas are active zones, while the blue areas are bleeds and safety zones. So, while both pink and blue need to be covered by your artwork or background, any text and important elements need to be confined to the pink areas. The template also displays the exact width that your spine should be, so make any adjustments needed to your cover spread dimensions and place the full-resolution image on the color-coded areas of the template. Due to variances in the binding process, borders or text can be chopped off or lost in a crease if they are too close to the edge of the book or the edge of the spine—hence, IngramSpark requires about a quarter inch of extra space (also called bleeds) around all outside edges of your cover spread. Save the combined template and cover spread as a new PDF file, then upload it to the "Cover File" box as you did with the interior file.

E-book File

IngramSpark requires that e-books be saved in ePUB format, the universal open-source file format for digital books. If your ePUB file is ready, upload it to the

"E-book File" box. If not, there are many ways to get your print manuscript digitized into a full flowing e-book file, both at home and through freelancers. IngramSpark offers a file conversion service for $0.60 per page; just select "Convert your PDF to ePUB with IngramSpark" from your Dashboard. You'll be prompted to provide your contact information and some metadata for your book, including a unique ISBN that you've assigned to the digital edition of your book. Once the conversion process is finished, your new ePUB file will be saved to your IngramSpark account.

Cover Image File

IngramSpark saves the easiest file for last. Your e-book cover image should be a JPG of just the front cover of your book, without bleeds. If you don't have an image like this saved, ask your designer to prepare one for you or crop it down from your full cover spread and save the file as a JPG. Finally, upload the JPG to the "Cover Image File" box.

Click the "Continue" button to enter the content validation phase, where Ingram-Spark internally scans your book files for errors or glitches. If any problems are discovered, IngramSpark will prompt you with how to correct them. It's normal to have to upload files a few times, especially when books contain images or special formatting. Once your files have passed the scanner, IngramSpark will prompt you to pay your upload fees for this title (remember that you can be refunded your print upload fees by ordering 50+ books within 60 days of this moment). Your upload is finished, and your book has been transmitted to Ingram's technical team, who will prepare your files for printing and binding! When processing is complete, you will be notified by e-mail to review an e-proof of your book. Once that step is complete, the status will change to "Available for printing/download" on your Dashboard.

ORDERS AND REPORTS

Ordering print runs

Now that your book's pages and cover have been formatted, uploaded, and accepted into the IngramSpark database, you have the power to print your book on demand. This means that you can customize the quantity of copies produced in each of your print runs to suit any situation. Traditional publishers generally use off-set printing, which binds a minimum of several thousand copies in each print run for a very cheap per unit cost; print-on-demand, however, does not impose quantity minimums, making it a flexible and financially feasible option for indie publishers who can't afford the investment of printing thousands of books at a time.

HINT: Even though retailers can access your book through Ingram's distribution channel, it's important to keep a steady personal stock of your book at all times. There's no worse feeling than getting a sudden rush of demand for your book, only to find yourself empty-handed and scrambling to fulfill orders.

To begin placing a print run order, go to your IngramSpark Dashboard and either click on the "Orders" tab near the top of the screen or click the "Order" button next to a recently uploaded title. The "Orders" tab will direct you to the "Orders Not Yet Submitted" page (this helps to keep you from accidentally creating duplicate orders); from there, use the menu on the left-hand side of the screen to create new orders, review past orders, manage your shipping addresses, or run a report on prerelease orders that have been placed for your book.

Before printing books that you intend to sell, I very strongly recommend that you order a single bound copy to proofread first (if you have multiple proofreaders, print a few copies so your readers can work on the text simultaneously). It's worth taking the extra time to get it right; cover art and page images can look very different in print from the way they do on a computer screen, and some formatting glitches can be tough to spot until they're seen on a printed page. No one wants to open up an entire box of books only to find that someone's name was misspelled in the acknowledgments or that a page is missing from the epilogue.

Your first step is to click the "Create New Order" link on the side menu. This will prompt you to check any titles you want to include in the order. Titles that are in the upload or revision process will be

■ NOTES:

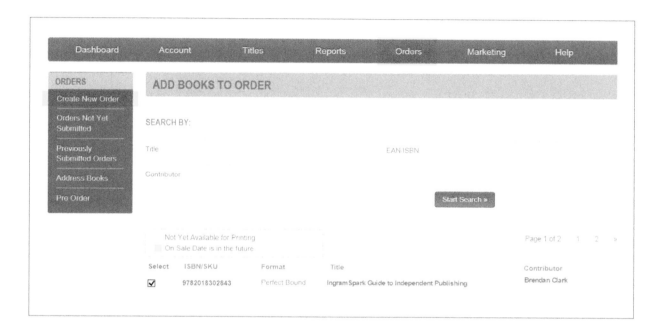

highlighted in blue, meaning they cannot be ordered yet; titles that have an on sale date in the future will be highlighted in yellow, meaning that you can either ship the print run ahead of the on sale date or put the order on hold as a preorder until the day the title is officially released. Since you can print multiple different titles on the same order, don't feel like you need to place separate orders for each individual title! Once you've checked the correct title(s), click the "Add Items to Order" button.

You will be taken to the "Edit Order" page, titled at the top with a unique ID number for your order. (If you clicked the "Order" button next to a recent title on the Dashboard, you would have been directed straight to this page.) Here, you can select the shipping address where the bound books should be delivered and the return address that should show on the box. If you are shipping the books to yourself, these addresses should be the same. You also have the option of shipping full orders of books to retailers or even individual customers; when you do this, the return address will identify you, the indie publisher, as the original shipper. Use this to fulfill distant orders quickly and efficiently, from the comfort of your own home.

Make sure your "Print Location" matches the correct form of currency, and enter a promo code if you have one from a special offer. Then, choose your preferred printing speed; standard time for a print run to be fully bound is five business days (economy), but for a slightly higher per unit printing cost you can expedite printing to two days (express) or one day (rush). Likewise, you can select a standard ground shipping speed (which can take around five days, depending on location), or expedite the shipment to two days or one day.

For each title you previously selected, enter a quantity of books to be printed; for the purposes of efficient shipping, the "Carton Qty" refers to the number of copies of that particular book that can be shipped in a single box. Once the quantities are correct, click the "Update Order" button on the bottom of the screen and the system will calculate the total cost of your order. This will include the per unit printing

HINT: Don't hit the back button right after finalizing your order! This can result in accidentally duplicating your order. Instead, use the gray taskbar to navigate back to the Dashboard or to another page in your IngramSpark interface.

cost of each book, multiplied by the quantity of each book ordered, plus a $1.50 handling fee and the cost of shipping (which is calculated based on weight, speed, and location).

Then, if all the information on the page looks correct, click the "Submit Order" button to be taken to the screen where you input payment details. Double-check the details of your order, then scroll down to the "Payment Method" drop-down menu (this will provide a list of all credit/debit cards you've saved to your account). Select the card you'd like to use, provide the card's security code, enter an optional purchase order number, enter your e-mail (twice), and click the "I Accept" button. This will finalize your order. Keep a record of the order number and confirmation code provided to you on the order confirmation page, in case you need the information later.

Once your order has been submitted, you can return to it by clicking "Orders" on the taskbar, then "Previously Submitted Orders," then the correct order number. At the bottom of the page you can find the status of each title (i.e. "Ready to print," "Printing," or "Shipped") and tracking numbers for any packages of books that have been shipped from the bindery.

Remember, ordering 50 or more copies of any title within 60 days of uploading the title earns you a refund of the upload fees for that title! Be smart about ordering

Saving Money on Your Print Runs

While print-on-demand cuts out print run minimums, you can still drastically improve the cost you pay per book by ordering larger quantities of books at a time. Shipping costs per unit shipped decrease the closer an order gets to a full carton, so it's much more efficient to bulk orders together. Printing individual titles at high enough quantities earns quantity discounts, which are applied to the cost of all copies of that title printed in that order (see below):

1–99 units = 10% off	1000–1499 units = 40% off
100–249 units = 15% off	1500–1999 units = 45% off
250–499 units = 25% off	2000+ units = 50% off
500–999 units = 35% off	

your print runs, and most importantly, be realistic about keeping supply consistent with demand. We all know the dreaded stereotype of the self-published author with a garage full to bursting with thousands of unsold books. Ordering print runs in large quantities will save money per unit, but you're not doing yourself any favors if those books never sell.

Reports

In addition to printing and distributing your titles, IngramSpark functions as an organizational resource for the business side of your publishing endeavors. Part of being a successful independently published author is keeping a watchful eye over the funds you've invested in a book project relative to the profits earned from sales of your book. Fortunately, all the sales data you could need for your print-on-demand titles and e-books are available at the click of a button.

From the Dashboard, click on the "Reports" tab near the top of the screen, then click on the type of information you're looking for. All reports prompt you to specify the period of time you need information for and the correct unit of currency. E-book Sales Report and Print Sales Report allow you to filter by particular ISBN, title, or author; use these to keep record of your sales through Ingram's distribution channels. Most reports can either be read in your web browser or sent to you via e-mail, except for the Billing Report, which must be transmitted by e-mail and details any money you've paid to IngramSpark. Similarly, Invoice and Transaction reports organize your account charges into individual invoices and an overall summary, respectively.

If you encounter any issues with your reports or if you need any questions answered not covered here, don't hesitate to contact the IngramSpark support team, reachable via [ingramsparksupport@ingramcontent.com].

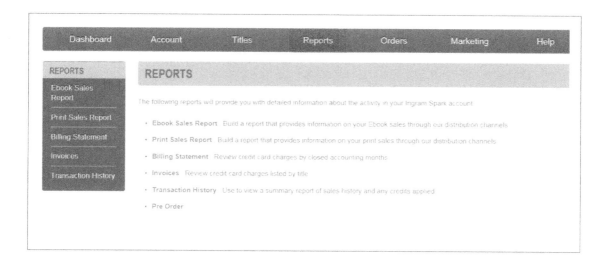

MARKETING

Breathe a deep sigh of relief; you've successfully developed your book into a product that can be printed, purchased, and enjoyed. But this immediately begs the question, who will buy your book? Certainly your immediate family and close friends will, because you've surely told them all about it. This simple word-of-mouth is the most basic and perhaps most important form of marketing; one person verbally introduces a new title to another person, then that person tells all of her friends about it, and so on.

Who else will buy your book? You can be sure not many people will go looking for your book if they've never heard of it before, and your book can't speak for itself (not in the literal sense, at least). As an independent publisher, your most daunting responsibility is reaching out to readers in the midst of an extremely oversaturated entertainment market. This chapter will explore strategies for encouraging more widespread awareness of your book through creative, targeted marketing.

Before we move on, it should be noted that the question "Who will buy your book?" operates on a deeper level than just identifying the demographic of readers most likely to purchase your book. It's a question that has hopefully been somewhere in the back of your mind throughout your creative process. Who is your intended audience? Who are you trying to deliver a message to? Keep your readers constantly in mind, and they will bring much-needed focus to both your craft and your marketing efforts.

Before you start publicizing your book, spend some time brainstorming a detailed marketing plan that includes print advertising, reading events, advertising through local publications, online social media blasts, reviewers whom you can ask for feedback, tradeshows relevant to the topic of your book, and niche audiences that might be interested in your book. If that seems overwhelming, try visualizing your reader.

When you visualize your reader, you can infer where they would be most likely to discover a new book like yours. Do they hang out in coffee shops and other public places? Put up some posters around town. Do they search for books online? Create a webpage for your book, make noise about it through online channels, and build a thorough online platform that will attract curious readers. Do they go to the local library or bookstore for recommendations? You'd better be sure the librarians and booksellers who work there are aware of your book, or at least have it on their shelves. Do they read book reviews in literary publications? Get your book reviewed, and if it's a good review, proudly publish the glowing recommendation where people can see it.

In the case of the latter two examples, the biggest obstacle is getting your book in the hands of someone in the trenches of the book industry. I recommend a little trick publishing houses have been using for years: give free books to people who make lots of book recommendations to the general public (i.e. booksellers, librarians, and reviewers). These professional bookworms often know about newly published titles before they've even hit the market because they've read books sent to them by publishers, making them uniquely positioned to build momentum for a particular title through self-perpetuating word-of-mouth. Time to get some padded envelopes and put this chain reaction to work for your book!

Advance Reader Copies (ARCs)

Remember those 50 copies I suggested that you print in order to recoup IngramSpark's title setup fees? If your publication date is still a ways off, one very effective use for those books is to give them to advance readers as galleys (also known as prepublication copies or ARCs). This might seem like a lot of books to give away for free, but even a small publishing house wouldn't bat an eyelash at mailing out 50 ARCs, considering their immense marketing potential.

Since they are sent out to advance readers several months before anyone is legally allowed to sell the title, ARCs are often marked "not for sale." Sometimes they are even sent out before the book has been fully edited and designed, meaning that typos and a plain cover are acceptable in ARCs; as such, readers are duly cautioned to not use direct quotes from the prepub version of the book. The main idea is to generate advance praise for your book and to get your book on the radar of people who will mention it to other potential readers right when it hits the shelves.

As an independent publisher, you don't have many of the advantages publishing houses bring to the table, including a known reputation for quality books and sales reps who talk up their favorite titles in discussions with retailers. What you can bring to the table are your local connection with booksellers and librarians in your regional area, the enthusiasm to convince readers that your book is worth a shot, and the persistence to follow up and ask for feedback.

Since people are most interested in books that are about or originate from their own local area, indie authors have the best chance of getting discovered close to home. So, make a list of retailers and libraries near you whom you can approach first, then plan to spread out your efforts as you go. Write a succinct, courteous, descriptive letter to the recipients of your ARCs asking them to read your book, include the letter with the book, and politely check back a couple months or so later to ask how

Use the back cover of an ARC, or Advance Reader Copy, to highlight plans for marketing the title. Also incorporate the overall specs including the pub date, trim, and page count.

they liked it. For local retailers and libraries, don't just drop in; call ahead and ask who is in charge of receiving new inventory, then ask when would be a convenient time for you to drop off a copy of your book. Cast your net wide enough, and you might win the fancy of a bookseller who will put your book in the unsuspecting hands of new readers over and over again.

Every time you interact with booksellers, librarians, or any of your advance readers, remember that you're not doing them a favor by giving them a book to read (if anything, they're doing you a favor by reading it). Don't be afraid to show your enthusiasm for your book, but be careful to not come off as obnoxious or evangelistic. Be appreciative, be friendly, be courteous, and most importantly, be respectful.

Once your readers have had enough time to sit down with your book, contact those whose opinions are meaningful to others (authors, booksellers, professionals in your field, editors, professional reviewers, etc) and ask them for feedback that you can use in your marketing. You can also pay to have your book reviewed by established publications such as *Kirkus Reviews* and *Foreword Magazine*; both are highly respected for the simple fact that these reviewers are notoriously harsh, meaning that even a mixed review from *Kirkus* or *Foreword* is something to be proud of. Once you've compiled a few positive blurbs for your book, copy/paste them into a sell sheet that includes your book's basic metadata, your bio, your website address, and a brief synopsis. Going forward, you can include this sell sheet in your mailings and/or anytime you need to efficiently communicate essential information about your book (including the fact that people love it).

Bear in mind that the practice of giving away (or hand selling) books to increase local buzz shouldn't necessarily stop after your book has been released. Get into the good habit of carrying a couple extra copies in your bag as you go about your daily business; you never know when you'll run into an acquaintance or random stranger who might be interested in your book, so be prepared. For improvised hand-selling opportunities to folks who use e-readers, print up business cards with a weblink they can use to download your e-book.

Promote Your Titles via IngramSpark

Another way that booksellers and librarians discover new books to add to their inventory is through trade catalogs they receive from publishers and distributors. A professional book buyer will sit down with these catalogs, full to bursting with blurbs and exciting new titles, and decide which titles will show up on their shelves next season. Wouldn't it be great if your book were in one of those catalogs, where

> **HINT:** Combining this strategy with sending ARCs is especially effective; two points of contact with book industry professionals are always better than one.

such literary-minded decision makers can find it? Fortunately, your established ally IngramSpark can help you here too. As the world's largest book distributor, Ingram issues its own series of catalogs to retailers and libraries—Ingram Advance Catalog (for adult fiction and nonfiction), Ingram Christian Advance Catalog (for books marketed to a primarily Christian audience), Ingram Children's Advance Catalog (for kids and young adult titles), and Ingram E-Central E-Newsletter (for digital titles).

From your Dashboard or Titles screens, you can select "Promote" to upload your book's metadata to Ingram's print publicity department (along with positive reviews you've collected from advance readers and some enticing flavor text). Your book will then be included in the next installment of your preferred catalog, all of which are issued to retailers and librarians periodically throughout the year.

Social Media

In addition to word-of-mouth marketing and print publicity, generating buzz on the digital landscape can bring your book to thousands of readers all over the world. Building and maintaining an online platform for your book and for yourself as an author is perhaps your best chance of achieving a widespread readership beyond your regional area. This extensive and time-consuming process extends

NOTES:

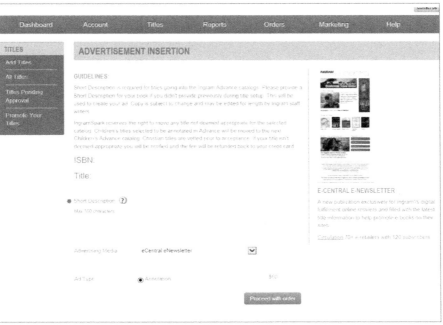

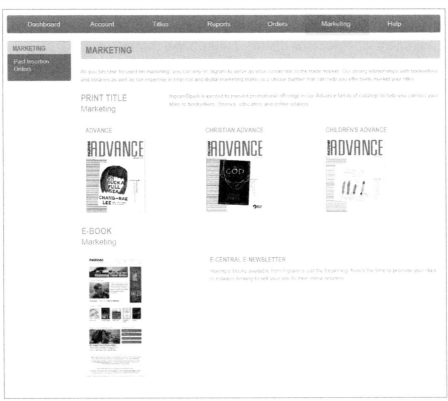

> **HINT:** When interacting online, remember to always be respectful instead of pushy, engaged in discussion rather than screaming your opinions from your little corner of the web.

from the nuts and bolts of having your book available for online purchase, to joining the online community of literary bloggers.

Before your book's official on sale date, you want online customers to be able to easily locate and purchase your book. Ingram's distribution channels will do some of this work for you by making your book discoverable through online book retailers. Be diligent about making sure those online listings are correct and functional. Try searching for your book with a search engine like Google; if it doesn't show up, you may need to make a website for your book and look into Search Engine Optimization. Once you do have a website up and running, be sure to include a hyperlink that takes your online visitors to a page where they can purchase your book, or provide them with easy instructions for ordering one directly from you.

Creating a Facebook page and a Twitter account for your book can open up many options for marketing your book. Be creative!

- Once you have some followers, offer signed copies of your book to any who preorder from a local bookstore.

- If you're still in the writing process or are writing a new book, let your followers submit artwork or ideas for character names for prizes.

- Create an events page for any reading events you have coming up and tweet about them

- Tweet, retweet, and generally interact with people online who share your interests, then suggest that they take a look at this cool title you just published independently.

- Once you've built a network with other writers and readers, you can reach out to people in their networks, and so on and so on.

Also, don't forget about Pinterest, Instagram, and especially YouTube. With a webcam or smartphone, you can film videos of yourself talking about your book and post them online as a sort of dialogue with your readership. Some authors even enlist the help of a video production company to create their own book trailers, which can be uploaded, shared, and disseminated to curious readers worldwide.

The vast macrocosm of bloggers on the Internet contains an immense community of literary reviewers, writers, and readers who share book recommendations in thousands of discussion threads over millions of websites, every second of every day. Entering into this community with just your book can feel like diving into the ocean, just to show the fish a seashell you found. Remember that you've got to start somewhere, and there's no wrong place to start.

Create a blog of your own, write a few posts about your writing process or the premise of your book or the factors that first inspired you to write, find some other bloggers who seem to share interests with you, comment on their posts, and watch your network start to grow. Blogging is all give and take; you've got to produce unique material and be reading and responding to others as well, in order to attract readers. Again, once that momentum gets going, your network will build on itself and you'll have a whole circle of online connections who can suggest your book to their connections, on and on.

Reading Events

Perhaps the most quintessential platform for pitching your book to prospective readers is the reading event, which gives authors the unique chance to connect with readers face-to-face. You can have a launch event on the day your book is released, or anytime within the first few months after your book hits store shelves. To get the ball rolling, contact your local bookstore or another public venue by phone or e-mail, then introduce yourself as an author hoping to schedule an event. Venues often fill their calendars several months in advance, so plan ahead and make contact well ahead of the time you'd ideally like to have your event.

Politely and briefly describe your book and the type of reading you have in mind— many authors opt for the time-honored formula of reading a few favorite passages and opening up the discussion for Q&A, while others present a multimedia slide-show or an activity that encourages audience participation. You can strengthen your case by describing positive feedback from reviewers, the other kinds of mar-keting you've invested in your book, and most importantly, your connections with the local community that would enable you to attract a large audience to your event. Once your venue has agreed to host you and set a calendar date for your event, start getting the word out to everyone you know!

On the day of your event, make sure your venue is well-stocked with your book and make sure plenty of copies are stacked up or put on display near the site of the read-ing (it's also wise to bring a few of your own extra copies, just in case). Providing refreshments, snacks, or promo giveaways is a nearly foolproof strategy for drawing complete strangers into your event; it's incredible how easily enticed people can be.

When you interact with potential readers at readings or signings, remember to be outgoing and engage people in conversation. A rehearsed lecture and choice paragraphs read aloud will certainly communicate to people what your book is about, but ultimately the best way to know you're talking about something that interests your readers is to ask for their questions and answer them. You never quite know where such a discussion will go—stay positive, focus on what inspires you to write, don't give away too much of the story, and go with the flow.

After your event, be sure to thank the audience for attending and thank the venue for hosting you. Most literary event programs are funded primarily by sales of books at their events, so encourage everyone who attends your event to support the venue by purchasing a copy of the book there; this means never ever tell people at events to buy your book online! Always offer to sign books for readers, but be sure to personally inscribe books only after they have been paid for.

From there, it's on to the next event! If you have the flexibility to travel, take your book on tour and give readings in different cities along the road. Everywhere you go, be constantly on the lookout for opportunities to introduce new readers to the book you've published.

■ ■ ■

While the world of self-publishing can boast of extravagant success stories where previously unknown authors have risen to national prominence, those examples are very much the exception, not the rule. In truth, it is monumentally difficult to establish a national readership as an independent author. Remember that your book is just one in millions, and you likely don't have the funds to invest as much into marketing as any publishing house would.

It can be easy to get discouraged, but don't give up! Building enough of a fan base to carry your book to the forefront of the book market requires an incredible amount of publicity and often a good bit of dumb luck as well. Fortunately, IngramSpark provides you with the tools and discoverability to prime your book for the recognition it deserves. From there, the more enthusiasm and persistence you devote to your book, the greater your ability to reach out to an entire world of readers.

I hope you've enjoyed this guided tour through the multilayered process of producing and distributing your books through IngramSpark. Now, it's time to take your next step as an informed, equipped independently published author. And IngramSpark will be there to help you every step of the way.

GLOSSARY

AGENCY PRICE: The price at which Apple sells the title through iTunes. All prices must be in dollar increments that end in .99, except if you set the price for $0 (i.e., free).

BARCODE: A machine-readable image on the back of books to indicate ISBN and possibly the price. Barcodes are required by many retailers for print products that they carry. This can be in the form of an EAN (European Article Number) barcode, used for books, or a UPC (Universal Product Code) barcode, used more commonly in the US for non-book products.

CONTENT: The chapters or other formal divisions of a book or e-book.

CONTRIBUTORS: Up to three contributors (e.g. authors, editors, illustrators, etc) may be identified with a book. These are saved and communicated to retailers via IngramSpark catalog information.

COPYRIGHT: A form of intellectual property, giving the creator of an original work exclusive rights to that work's publication, distribution, and adaptation for a certain time period. After the time period, the work is said to enter the public domain. For information on US copyright laws, visit www.copyright.gov.

DESCRIPTION: This brief description of the book will be communicated to distribution partners who wish to describe and market the book on their website(s) and to their customers. We recommend that you provide a book description for all new books to assist booksellers in presenting your books to their customers. The book description should be at least 40 characters, but should not exceed 4,000 characters including spaces. In addition, no HTML tagging, bullets, or other special formatting should be embedded.

DIGITAL RIGHTS MANAGEMENT (DRM): A system or technology used to place limitations (in regards to access or copying) onto digital content (books, movies, music, etc). A publisher or author, not the retailer, determines the level of restrictions applied to it. This includes how many times content can be downloaded for a single purchase, and the number of devices (computers, readers, etc) to which the content can be transferred. DRM is usually administered by those that convert or sell the content.

DIRECT STORE PROGRAMS: A web portal from e-retailers, such as Apple and Barnes & Noble, where you can upload your content and then post for sale only in their online store.

DISTRIBUTOR: A party that handles all fulfillment, credit, and collections on behalf of a publisher. A distributor looks for an exclusive agreement with the publisher within geographic areas and types of markets and, therefore, is likely to stock all titles from a publisher in their warehouse. In the case of the book industry, a distributor would sell to retailers and to wholesalers.

DOWNLOAD: The act of transferring a file from the Internet to your computer or mobile device.

E-RETAILER (ONLINE RETAILER): An online retailer that sells books, both physical and digital, and often other related merchandise to readers. E-retailers source their products from various players in the supply chain including publishers, wholesalers, distributors, and fulfillment companies.

EDITION: Version of a work. A new edition means that there have been a series of corrections and/or a new feature added (such as a preface, appendix, or additional content), or that the content has been revised.

ELECTRONIC BOOK/E-BOOK: Digital equivalent of a conventional printed book. E-books are read on personal computers, smartphones, or readers. There are many formats available; some can be used on multiple devices while others are only available on certain devices.

EPUB (.EPUB): A format from the International Digital Publishing Forum, ".epub" is the file extension of an XML format for digital books and publications. EPUB reflows content, so that text can be optimized for the display screen being used at the time.

FILE TRANSFER PROTOCOL (FTP): A way to transfer files to and from websites without using a browser. Usually requires FTP client software.

FULFILLMENT: The process of filling orders. Fulfillment firms usually provide storage, pick, pack, and ship services for publishers. A company can also offer file creation, storage, and delivery to online retailers or e-books. Could also be called Digital Distributor.

IMPRINT: An imprint is a trade name used by a publisher to identify a line of books or a publishing branch within the publishing organization. An imprint is distinguished from a corporate name in that it does not represent an entity with a corporate life of its own. The imprint appears on all books produced in the line. Imprints are optional and not required.

ISBN (INTERNATIONAL STANDARD BOOK NUMBER): A unique 13-digit number provided by your country's ISBN agency and assigned by the publisher to identify a particular format, edition, and publisher of a book. ISBNs are used worldwide as a unique identifier for each book title/format combination. They are used to simplify the distribution and purchase of books throughout the global supply chain.

.JPG OR .JPEG (JOINT PHOTOGRAPHIC EXPERTS GROUP): An image file format ideal for digital images with lots of colors, such as photographs and the cover image for your book.

KEYWORDS: Single words or short phrases that describe your book and help improve search results.

MARKET (CHANNEL): Bookselling outlets are often grouped by the type of customers they service. Examples include traditional bookstores (known as trade), big-box stores (e.g. Costco, Target, Wal-Mart), religious bookstores, gift stores, libraries, and educational accounts. E-commerce or sales through an online channel are another market channel.

METADATA: Details about your title that booksellers and buyers need to know. It includes details specific to a particular form of the book (e.g. price, hardcover, paperback, publication date) as well as general information that may apply to all forms of your work (e.g. author, description, table of contents).

OFFSET PRINTING: Printing on a traditional printing press where many copies of a book are produced at one time.

ONIX: The international standard for representing and communicating book industry product information via electronic form. This XML standard is commonly used by retailers, distributors, and wholesalers to communicate with each other about books that are available for sale.

ON SALE DATE: The date to determine when a book may be sold by retail partners.

PAGE COUNT: Page count is the total number of pages in the book, including blanks and front matter. The total number of pages must be evenly divisible by 2.

PDF (.PDF): A file format developed by Adobe to allow the creation and sharing of documents that will look and print the same on any machine.

PRINT ON DEMAND (POD): Printing, usually from a digital file to a digital printer. In this case, the physical book is only printed when it is ordered. The exact number of copies ordered is what is printed. No extra copies are kept on warehouse shelves.

PUBLICATION DATE: The date on which a retail consumer or library may take possession of a product.

PUBLISHER: The entity that owns the legal right to make the product available. This can be the same entity as the author, a company formed by the author or a group of authors to publish their own works, a self-publishing service provider that assists the author in bringing the book to market, or a traditional publishing company that purchases the right to publish a work from an author.

REPRINT: A new batch of printed copies without substantial changes.

RETAILER: A store that sells books, and often other related merchandise, to readers. Retailers source their products from various players in the supply chain including publishers, wholesalers, and distributors.

RETURNS: Historically, publishers grant booksellers the right to return unwanted and/or overstocked copies of books. These books are considered "returnable." As books are returned, booksellers charge publishers for the cost (i.e. their purchase price) of any books returned and expect to be reimbursed. The cost of returned books is either deducted or netted against the proceeds of book sales of the publishers' titles in the month returns are shipped to the publisher. IngramSpark supports standard industry conventions by allowing publishers to designate whether or not their titles can be returned. The publisher can make this designation at the time of initial title setup.

NON-RETURNABLE: Select this designation if you do not want to allow your titles to be sold on a returnable basis. IngramSpark will not accept returns from booksellers for any title so designated.

YES-DELIVER: Select this designation if you want to allow your titles to be sold on a returnable basis and you would like to receive a physical copy of the book returned. IngramSpark does not guarantee the condition of the book being returned.

RETURNS TO US ADDRESSES: If you select this option, you will be charged for the current wholesale cost of each book returned, plus a $2.00 per book shipping and handling charge.

RETURNS TO NON-US/INTERNATIONAL ADDRESSES: If you select this option, you will be charged for the current wholesale cost of each book returned, plus a $20.00 per book shipping and handling charge.

YES-DESTROY: Select this designation if you want to allow your titles to be sold on a returnable basis and you would not like to receive a physical copy of the book upon its return. If you select this option, you will be charged only for the current wholesale cost of each book returned. No shipping and handling fees will apply. IngramSpark will destroy any returned books that it receives if this option is selected. IngramSpark allows you to change the return designations of a title at any time after initial title submission with 45 days prior written notice. You have the ability to change the return designation from your Dashboard. Select "Edit" and progress through to step number 4 of the process. Publishers may check the sales and returns activity of any or all titles at any time by logging into our publisher secure website.

STATUS: Indicates the availability of the book. The book industry uses terms, such as forthcoming (going to be published in the future), active (available for purchase now), and publication cancelled (item will not be published now or in the future). When telling customers about your title, you may be asked to supply this information.

SUBJECT: The IngramSpark distribution network partners use Subjects to categorize books. These categories briefly describe the content of a book. Retailers, distributors, and libraries require you to select at least one subject.

SUGGESTED RETAIL PRICE: Publishers determine the suggested retail list price on all titles in all markets. If pricing is not submitted the title will appear as unavailable for sale in that market.

TERRITORY RIGHT: The rights of a distributor, granted by the producer or supplier, to sell a product in a particular geographical area.

TITLE: The title information placed in this field will be used for all reporting and reseller catalog communications (where appropriate).

TRADE: Refers to traditional bookselling channels including independent bookstores (e.g. a single store, a local group of stores) and chain bookstores (e.g. Barnes & Noble, Hastings, Books-a-Million).

TRADE DISCOUNT: An amount or rate by which the catalog, list, or suggested retail price of an item is reduced when sold to a reseller. The trade discount reflects the reseller's profit margin

TRADING TERMS (AKA PUBLISHER DISCOUNT): Each publisher will need to set trading terms with each customer. When selling to distributors, wholesalers, or retail bookstores, you are expected to quote a price that allows them to resell the book and make money on that sale. First, you will set the retail price (the price the reader buys at) for each geographic market in which the product is available. This can be expressed in the local currency or in USD. Then you will set the price at which the distributor, wholesaler, or retailer would purchase from you.

WHOLESALER: A business that obtains books from publishers and their appointed distributors in order to fulfill orders for retailers and libraries. They offer non-exclusive distribution to publishers. Wholesalers will stock certain quantities of titles, but will usually not warehouse your entire inventory. Wholesalers meet customer requests for packaging books across a set of publishers and deliver the goods quickly to meet retailer or library needs.

Sources: Ingram, Bowker, IBPA, and Lulu from the uPublishu Conference at BookExpo America, May 2013.

INDEX

CPSIA information can be obtained
at www.ICGtesting.com
Printed in the USA
LVOW05s1455130317
527030LV00024B/325/P